# MELVILLE'S
## *Shorter Tales*

HERMAN MELVILLE

From a painting by Asa W. Twitchell

# MELVILLE'S
## *Shorter Tales*

*

*by Richard Harter Fogle*

UNIVERSITY OF OKLAHOMA PRESS : NORMAN

By RICHARD HARTER FOGLE

*Melville's Shorter Tales* (Norman, 1960)
*Hawthorne's Fiction: The Light and the Dark*
(Norman, 1952)
(Ed.) *John Keats: Selected Poetry and Letters*
(New York, 1951)
*The Imagery of Keats and Shelley* (Chapel Hill, 1949)

*The publication of this work has been aided by a grant
from Tulane University*

LIBRARY OF CONGRESS CATALOG CARD NUMBER: 60–7741

*To my wife*
*Catherine Cox Fogle*

# *Acknowledgments*

I AM INDEBTED to Jay Leyda's edition of *The Complete Stories of Herman Melville* (New York, Random House, 1949) for texts, the ordering of Melville's shorter tales, and valuable information and suggestions furnished by Mr. Leyda's introduction and notes. My interpretations have doubtless drawn upon the work of many other scholars and critics, especially F. O. Matthiessen, Newton Arvin, Ellery Sedgwick, and Richard Chase. Their intention, however, is to owe most to Melville himself.

I am happy to acknowledge the generous assistance of the Tulane University Council on Research in the preparation and publication of this book. Two sections of it, Chapters II and X, were printed originally in *Tulane Studies in English,* and Chapter IX, "The Encantadas," is republished from *Nineteenth-Century Fiction,* Vol. X (1955), 34-52, by permission of the University of California Press.

*Richard Harter Fogle*

New Orleans, Louisiana
October 24, 1959

# Contents

ix

# MELVILLE'S
## *Shorter Tales*

I

# Melville's Tales

THE WORLD of Melville is immeasurable and mysterious. It is *one* world, but of a complex unity beyond the mind of man to fathom. All things are interrelated, yet in so vast and intricate a labyrinth that monism and pluralism are in their consequences almost alike, meeting in a common complexity.[1] It is man's problem, and certainly Melville's problem, that he is a teleological animal. He seeks in this world for benevolence and intelligible purpose: he looks for God to take his side and is dismayed to find indifference. Melville is a religious-minded agnostic, a rationalist distrustful of reason, an indefatigable seeker uncertain of the ultimate ends of his search. All these are excellent things for a writer to be, and all are rather wearing. For Melville the world is meaning, and physical reality is a sacrament.[2] Meaning, however, is multiple, and not to be lightly read. The "tragedy of mind," in Sedgwick's

[1] This view of Melville is more fully discussed in Mary E. Dichmann, "Absolutism in Melville's *Pierre*," *PMLA (Publications of the Modern Language Association)*, Vol. LXVII (1952), 702–15; and below, pp. 73, 75, 87, 93–94, 97, 114–15.

[2] See F. O. Matthiessen, *American Renaissance* (New York, 1941), 248–52; Charles Feidelson, Jr., *Symbolism and American Literature* (Chicago, 1953), 176 f.

phrase,[3] is man's insatiable desire to read the unreadable. It might be added, perhaps, that there is a bitter comedy in his penchant for jumping at conclusions. Ultimately Melville's world is neither good nor bad. There is something to be said for it, however; it is total, it has dignity and scope, and the men in it are real.

Given this world, the purpose of the tales as of all Melville's fiction is to penetrate as deeply as possible into its metaphysical, theological, moral, psychological, and social truths. Negatively he means to refute the shallow and conventional notions of his times. He thinks it his business to provide a spacious and undivided wisdom, and he makes no clear distinction between art and teaching, representation and statement. He partly shares in the general nineteenth-century distrust of plot and external action, and he is fond of apologue and parable. In these tales he wishes to conceal, however, his direct purposes,[4] for artistic, personal, financial, and sometimes humorous reasons. Further, his state of mind at the time of writing is morbid, his sensibility heightened to the point of disease,[5] and it must go veiled in public in sheer self-preservation. These concealments cause an interesting situation, in conflict with his other purposes of being free, uncommitted, impartially able to record the visible truth.

The form of Melville's tales is determined by the direc-

[3] William Ellery Sedgwick, *Herman Melville: The Tragedy of Mind* (Cambridge, Mass., 1944).

[4] See Lawrance Thompson, *Melville's Quarrel with God* (Princeton, 1952). Mr. Thompson suggests, however, a more systematic concealment and a simpler motive for it than I am able to accept.

[5] See Newton Arvin, "The Lee Shore," in *Herman Melville* (New York, 1950), 195–215. There is, however, general agreement about Melville's state of mind at this time.

4

tion and quality of his thought, in which man as the seeker for knowledge is always pitted against a finally inscrutable reality, and this conflict is further complicated by the need for concealment. Since every man sees reality differently, partially, and from his own point of view, the tales are often ambiguous, as are the shifting clouds and ranges of the Berkshires in "The Piazza." The march of Fate and the quest for truth are embodied in heavy, repetitive movement, as in "Bartleby" and "Benito Cereno." Rhetorical repetition and chorus in the comments of the narrative character have the same effect of a relentless closing-in: the refrain, for example, of "Poor, poor Jimmy Rose!" or the "Oh, noble cock!" of "Cock-a-Doodle-Doo." Strangely mingled with this heavy, straightforward movement is an occasional appearance of leisurely digressiveness, in keeping with the mystery and complexity of Melville's world, and with his ceaseless aspirations to explore it. These digressions are sometimes only apparent and are finally revealed as functional parts of a larger design, as in "Benito Cereno," or, on the other hand, they are merely added attractions to slight stories or sketches like "I and My Chimney."

A number of tales are dialectically arranged in what Jay Leyda has aptly called diptychs,[6] or two-paneled structures, as if to say, "Look here upon this picture and on this." Such are "The Two Temples," "Poor Man's Pudding and Rich Man's Crumbs," and "The Paradise of Bachelors and the Tartarus of Maids." This device of structure has two causes. First, Melville is refuting incom-

[6] *The Complete Stories of Herman Melville*, ed. by Jay Leyda (New York, 1949), xx.

plete and shallow optimism, or mere simple-mindedness, by demonstrating that good and evil exist alike, by showing the same object in different perspectives. Second, and correspondingly, Melville's is a world of violent contrast, the dimpling water and the shark beneath,[7] a world full of ironies which come of man's presumption in taking the part of life that he sees for the whole of it.

The tales have either the pattern of the quest, in which a seeker actively pursues truth, as in "The Piazza" or "Cock-a-Doodle-Doo," or the naturally converse situation of a man's being thrust into circumstances which dismay and baffle but conclude by educating him, as for instance the lawyer-narrator of "Bartleby." The quest and its object are represented primarily in visual terms, and thus the problem arises of point of view, alike mental and physical.

Clearly, Melville's chief intention was to get across what he had to say. *Moby Dick* shows that he has no objection to mixing his genres,[8] and his handling of Ishmael indicates that he is willing to sacrifice consistency in order to achieve fullness. He is no Henry James, to delight in the conditions of his craft. Like Jacob, he is willing, he

[7] "Beholding the tranquil beauty and brilliancy of the ocean's skin, one forgets the tiger heart that pants beneath it; and would not willingly remember, that this velvet paw but conceals a remorseless fang" (*Moby Dick*, chap. 114). Cf. Keats, "Epistle to John Hamilton Reynolds":

> . . . I saw
> Too far into the sea, where every maw
> The greater on the less feeds evermore.

[8] *Moby Dick* cannot be limited to any single kind; it has been called a drama and an epic, and one might well think of it as a prose poem.

says, "to wrestle with the angel, Art," but it remains a wrestling match and not a love-match. Nevertheless, the limitations of the tale force him into a tighter compass, and the pattern of the quest demands a visual emphasis and focus. Except in "The Bell-Tower," the tales avoid the spacious omniscient third person, and even in the broad survey of the islands of "The Encantadas," Melville works carefully outward from a visual center and point of vantage, the towering Rock Rodondo.

The problem of point of view gives Melville trouble, partly from the social responsibilities which he accepts in dealing with it. He has particular difficulty with the "I" narrator. The intrusion-of-the-author method is after all not the easy, primitive way of telling a story; its development is relatively recent and has its significant beginnings no farther back than Fielding. It is not merely an expedient and a convenience but a burden as well. The author must act as a witty and graceful master of ceremonies, and this Melville was not prepared to be, lacking as he was in a sense of his place in society, or of society as a real and permanent fabric of manners.

His early escape to sea was both literally and symbolically important. Society held little for him, and he could not assume the position of man of the world as could Thackeray, Trollope, or even (if one may say so) George Eliot. His world is too wide, his interest not in manners, and as a free man committed to nothing, as Bulkington forever clawing off lee shores, he has too little contact with his social audience. In the tales his tone is usually too violent, too tragic, too apocalyptic for his material. He is most successful in "Benito Cereno," where the action suits him, and where he is able at the same time to enter into Captain Delano and to be stimulated by the irony of Delano's miscomprehensions. Lacking this sympathy, in "Bartleby" he is forced to make the narrator satirize himself in order to convey his meaning. In "I and My Chimney" and "The Apple-Tree Table" he exaggerates the type to the point of caricature. His current, in fact, is generally too heavy for the conductor in these stories; there is insufficient "objective correlative" for the underlying dark and dangerous stuff of his emotions. His joviality is a little excessive, a little false, a little defensive. His persistent punning, which is often in Melville a method of metaphor and a sign of relation, is in the tales an illustration of Coleridge's theory that the pun is an outlet for suppressed anger and contempt:[9] in this case contempt for the reader of *Putnam's* and *Harper's* in the 1850's.

The use of the "I" narrator, however, is a way of establishing the point of view as an actual vision of objects. Whether the same end could have been better achieved it is useless here to inquire. Melville's method is, briefly, to seek first a point of vantage, and then also to view his object in different perspectives and relationships. Sometimes there is no point of vantage, and we are left with various insights but no central point of view. The approach in "The Encantadas" is deductive. One mounts the lofty Rock Rodondo (a feat which Melville tells us is possible only to the imagination). From here the eye can sweep the islands, then move and concentrate on each in turn. In "I and My Chimney," however, the great chim-

9 E.g., in Coleridge's *Shakespearean Criticism*, ed. by T. M. Raysor (Cambridge, Mass., 1930), I, 22.

MELVILLE'S TALES

ney which is the object of the story can never be seen as a whole. The narrator views its base in the cellar and digs about in its foundations; he looks at it from various sides and angles, which he is able to do because it passes through every chamber in the house; and finally he observes it at its heavenly level, emerging from the roof. "Temple No. 1" is a study in planes and perspective. The narrator mounts steadily from chamber to chamber, sometimes strangely lighted by "Gothic windows or richly dyed glass." He passes up a "Jacob's ladder of lofty steps," until he reaches at last a "small, round window," from which he has a comprehensive view of the interior of the church and the morning service that is going on. There is no glass in the window, which is really a ventilator for hot air, but it is covered by fine-woven wire, an obstacle which is like the minister's black veil in Hawthorne's story in its influence on the vision. "That wire-woven screen had the effect of casting crape upon all I saw. Only by making allowances for the crape could I gain a right idea of the scene disclosed."

The objects of Melville's vision are microcosms, complex and full. He is "transcendental" in his implicit acceptance of the doctrine of all in each, and of correspondences between the visible and the invisible worlds. In the novels his ships, the *Arcturus,* the *Neversink,* and the *Pequod,* are self-contained, complete worlds, as is the old *San Dominick* in "Benito Cereno" of the tales. The law office of "Bartleby," the attic of "The Apple-Tree Table," extend in meaning far beyond themselves. One instance, however, is sufficient to illustrate: the Rock Rodondo of "The Encantadas" group.

9

This rock is both vantage point and center. "Ere ascending," says Melville, "to gaze abroad upon the Encantadas, this sea-tower itself claims attention. It is visible at the distance of thirty miles . . . ." He approaches it carefully, a little before dawn. "The twilight was just enough to reveal every striking point, without tearing away the dim investiture of wonder"—the doctrine this of the Romantic picturesque in its combination of distinctness and unifying imaginative haze.

The rock rises from the sea in regular layers or strata, which suggest to Melville a stratified hierarchy of order and degree. It is crowded with sea birds, a different species on every level. On the lowest are penguins, who deserve their lowly place, for they are "the most ambiguous and least lovely creature yet discovered by man." The penguins stand all around the rock like caryatids, supporting the next level above them, upon which rest gray pelicans, "woe-begone regiments." "As we still ascend from shelf to shelf, we find the tenants of the tower serially disposed in order of their magnitude . . . :—thrones, princedoms, powers, dominating one above another in senatorial array." The emphasis upon order and hierarchy is unmistakable. High above all is "a white angelic thing,"[10] "a beauteous bird, from its bestirring whistle of musical invocation, fitly styled the 'Boatswain's Mate.' "

This pattern is supplied with aesthetic design and organic continuity by the intermingled presence of the stormy petrel on every level, "sprinkled over all, like an ever-repeated fly in a great piece of broidery." All levels

[10] But contrast the sky-hawk, the bird of heaven, dragged down with the rebellious *Pequod* (*Moby Dick*, chap. 135).

are swarming with life: "as the eaves of any old barn or abbey are alive with swallows, so were all these rocky ledges with unnumbered sea-fowl." There are, in fact, in the Rock Rodondo three elements of structure: hierarchical order—the high, the middle, and the low, from the angelic Boatswain's mate to the misshapen penguin; the interfusion of parts which is furnished by the omnipresent petrel; and the fullness, variety, and profusion suggested by the swarming birds. Melville's rock is a vision of complex organic unity in its reconciliation of opposing elements; it allows in the strata for firm outline, and succeeds also in expressing the vital interblending of organic relationships. The further element of fine excess and profusion, taken along with the "dim investiture of wonder," indicates a Romantic version of unity.

Melville remarks that the rock is the aviary of ocean, a compendium of the "Natural History of strange sea-fowl." The phrase suggests both the general and individual, and, in fact, while using the resources, he avoids the pitfall of the transcendental all-in-each, the trap of the unwary dealer in microcosms and macrocosms. This trap is simply the literal identification by which the each and the all are the same, and which accounts for some shortcomings in Whitman and Emerson. Melville, in the Rock Rodondo at least, preserves the object's limits, and its unique trait. For this is the world of the sea, which is a way of life and an aspect but not life itself.[11] The symbol reaches and extends far out, but it has at length its boundaries; its potentialities are not limitless. "Though Ro-

[11] See Matthiessen, *American Renaissance*, 289–90, for Melville's contrast of sea and land.

dondo be terra firma, no land-bird ever lighted on it. Fancy a red-robin or a canary there! What a falling into the hands of the Philistines, when the poor warbler should be surrounded by such locust-flights of strong bandit birds, with long bills cruel as daggers."

The tales are very uneven in quality. One should say the worst of them,[12] and combat the natural tendency to overrate them in proportion as they were underrated in the past. When every qualification has been made, Melville is still not a craftsman in the ordinary meaning of the term. He remains a Romantic apostle of the grand unfinished, the all-or-nothing man of the one stroke. He is too heavy for the delicate fabric of the kind of tale he is trying to write; what he really has to say is at odds with the limits he has chosen to observe. There is an unclosed gap between the surface of these tales and what Ahab calls "the little lower layer." "Benito Cereno" alone is a complete artistic triumph, if I may venture to disagree with some very weighty critical opinion. The fine "Encantadas" are marred by the story of the Chola widow. Even the wonderfully suggestive "Bartleby" is on the surface an uneasy, labored joke; and the interesting "Lightning-Rod Man" could strike an intelligent general reader only as

---

[12] ". . . few of the tales themselves are anything but thin, pale, insubstantial, and fatally easy to forget. There is something tasteless in doing more than mention such painfully concocted and convictionless pieces, artistically speaking, as 'Cock-a-Doodle-Doo!,' 'The Lightning-Rod Man,' 'The Fiddler,' 'The Bell-Tower,' and 'Poor Man's Pudding'" (Arvin, *Herman Melville*, 235). The present work will clearly have to do without sympathy from Mr. Arvin—which is a matter for regret. He speaks here for artistic integrity. I think, however, that he has reacted too vigorously against certain exaggerations of the value of Melville's later fiction.

ludicrous. To respect these tales at their full value, one must have respected Melville to begin with. Yet at worst they are transformed by Melville's brooding and contemplative intelligence, indefatigably exploring all facets and perspectives, as it steadily searches for the full vision of his object.

# II

# *"Bartleby"*

THE NARRATOR of "Bartleby" is one of Melville's bachelors,[1] a man uncommitted to life. "I am a man," he says,
"who, from his youth upwards, has been filled with a
profound conviction that the easiest way of life is the
best." A successful lawyer, he has nothing to do with the
turbulence of courts; he is one of those who "in the cool
tranquillity of a snug retreat, do a snug business among
rich men's bonds, and mortgages, and title-deeds." "All
who know me," he remarks, "consider me an eminently
*safe* man." The meaning of "safe" is more than single; the
narrator seeks safety for himself, too. With the aid of
prudence and method, he has fair hopes of gliding through
the world immune and untouched. Upon this man is
unleashed strange Bartleby, the nihilist scrivener, as a
*memento mori* and a *memento mali.* Live and let live is
the narrator's motto. He gets on comfortably with his two
clerks by wisely overlooking their faults, and he does his
best to pass over the faults and the ills of Bartleby. This,
however, is impossible. He is forced at last to see Bartleby

[1] A "bachelor" in Melville's fiction is a man who has not wedded
reality, a man who sees half of life but not the whole. Everyone who
achieves success is a bachelor, since he can only do so by closing
his eyes to the realities which make success impossible. See below,
pp. 46f., 50–51, 105, 132 f.

steadily and see him whole—a human being irremediably wrecked, for whom nothing can be done.[2]

To deal with Bartleby, he tries various interesting expedients. He will humor and befriend him, and thus "cheaply purchase a delicious self-approval." On the other hand, Bartleby's passiveness drives his employer at times into a perverse longing to stir him to new opposition. Later the narrator is forced to conclude that he can do nothing for his doomed clerk: "I might give alms to his body; but his body did not pain him; it was his soul that suffered, and his soul I could not reach." Pity, which had been not without pleasure, is now painful because hopeless. There is nothing for it but to get rid of Bartleby, which the narrator characteristically tries to manage by masterly inaction, by *assuming* that Bartleby will go quietly. This does not serve, and he is almost tempted to violence, from which he is saved by the prudent reflection that charity is the best policy. "Mere self-interest . . . should . . . prompt all beings to charity and philanthropy."[3]

He then resorts to a humorous fatalism, in which he conceives it his mission in life to furnish Bartleby with office room; but this soon proves impracticable. Bartleby's behavior causes too much remark, and his benefactor is in danger of scandal. "At last I was made aware that through all the circle of my professional acquaintance, a

[2] The relation between the narrator and Bartleby is essentially the same as the relation between Captain Delano and Benito Cereno.

[3] " 'It's a mutual, joint-stock world, in all meridians. We cannibals must help these Christians' " (*Moby Dick*, chap. 13). This is a pervasive theme in Melville. It should be pointed out, however, that to Melville to be in love and charity with one's neighbors is no final answer to man's difficulties; it is only a sensible expedient in carrying on a bad but inescapable business.

whisper of wonder was running round, having reference to the strange creature I kept at my office." The situation is too much to handle; unwilling to use force, he moves his office instead, leaving Bartleby to be dealt with by the new tenants. This move also fails to answer; he cannot settle down to business, is driven to wander. "So fearful was I of being again hunted out by the incensed landlord and his exasperated tenants, that, surrendering my business . . . for a few days, I drove about the upper part of the town and through the suburbs, in my rockaway; crossed over to Jersey City and Hoboken, and paid fugitive visits to Manhattanville and Astoria." In the end it is the landlord's "energetic, summary disposition" which causes Bartleby to be arrested and consigned to The Tombs.

There the amiable narrator visits him, hopeless but decent in observance. Bartleby shall have every possible comfort; but he will accept nothing. The narrator, like Captain Delano in a parallel scene in "Benito Cereno," reminds Bartleby of the beauty and strength which can be found in living nature.[4] "See," he says, "it is not so sad a place as one might think. Look, there is the sky, and here is the grass." To this Bartleby replies only, "I know

4 " 'But the past is passed; why moralize upon it? Forget it. See, yon bright sun has forgotten it all, and the blue sea, and the blue sky; these have turned over new leaves.'
" 'Because they have no memory,' he dejectedly replied; 'because they are not human.'
" 'But these mild trades that now fan your cheek, do they not come with a human-like healing to you? Warm friends, steadfast friends are the trades.'
" 'With their steadfastness they but waft me to my tomb, señor,' was the foreboding response" ("Benito Cereno").

where I am." Bartleby dies soon after; refusing to eat, he simply dries up, as it were, and blows away. The last words of the story are, "Ah, Bartleby! Ah, humanity!"— a universal conclusion. To the narrator his poor clerk has been an everlasting sign: there is evil in the world, and irremediable suffering, which good will cannot touch, nor good judgment avoid. "There are some ills that are cureless."

The narrator's two clerks, Turkey and Nippers, are remarkably interesting in a number of ways. These two are partly Dickens caricatures and partly jocular solar myths. The red-faced Turkey is a model worker in the morning but inclined to be obstreperous after lunch. "At such times, too, his face flamed with augmented blazonry, as if cannel coal had been heaped on anthracite." Like the sun, he rises to the zenith at noon and blazes in glory, then gradually wanes until 6:00 P.M. Nippers, on the other hand, "a whiskered, sallow, and upon the whole, rather piratical-looking young man," is nervous and testy in the morning, but in the afternoon comparatively mild. One thinks of Sir Gawaine, whose strength grew steadily till midday and then declined.

Turkey (Turkey red? swelling like a turkey gobbler?) and Nippers (the crab's claws) are quite exactly *humors* characters, immemorially comic figures. Turkey is sanguine, plethoric; Nippers is between the hot and dry choleric and the cold and dry of melancholy. Each is a half-man whom the shrewd narrator takes and uses for what he is. Turkey, plethoric, takes on too much and destroys his balance when he drinks his lunch, "as if cannel coal had been heaped on anthracite." Nippers is perpetually hungry and unsatisfied; the claws of the crab reach out. "I always deemed him the victim of two evil powers—ambition and indigestion." He grinds his teeth audibly over casual mischances; he is continually readjusting his desk to suit himself, without ever succeeding. "In short, the truth of the matter was, Nippers knew not what he wanted. Or, if he wanted anything, it was to be rid of a scrivener's table altogether."

Turkey is an Englishman, Nippers an American, and Melville makes them national types according to the mythology of the nineteenth century in which the beefy, stolid English John Bull stands over against the lean and restless Yankee.[5] Turkey—at least until noon—"knows his place." As "a dependent Englishman" he has a "natural civility and deference." His clothes are disreputable, since he cares little for appearances.[6] His employer remarks that he once presented Turkey with an overcoat, but the result was unfortunate. "It made him insolent. He was a man whom prosperity harmed." Nippers is an aspiring ward politician who sometimes offends his employer by bringing his clients into the office. On the other hand, he "was not deficient in a gentlemanly sort of deportment," and, moreover, was "always dressed in a gentlemanly sort of way; and so, incidentally, reflected credit upon my chambers."

[5] As, for example, in Emerson's *English Traits*, Hawthorne's *English Notebooks*, and Melville's *White-Jacket*. The captain of the *Samuel Enderby*, who is directly compared with the American Ahab *(Moby Dick*, chap. 100), is the representative Englishman, who stands for common-sense materialism at its best.

[6] "It is a thing which every sensible American should learn from every sensible Englishman, that glare and glitter, gimcracks and gewgaws, are not indispensable to domestic solace-ment" (Melville, "The Paradise of Bachelors").

Turkey and Nippers together, then, form an allegory of the English and American national characters, their virtues and their faults. They have no really vital function in the story of "Bartleby." Vis-à-vis Bartleby and the narrator, they do, however, have a more fundamental relationship than entertaining background alone. The narrator is toward them a kind of God; he knows them thoroughly and bears with them. He accepts their imperfect services because he accepts them as imperfect men and expects no better. They, in their turn, are not contented but rub along somehow. They bear the yoke without galling their necks unduly. There is a convention between them and their employer, an understanding by which they bear and forbear. Bartleby, however, is an extremist, and is more than his shrewd and moderate god can cope with.

Bartleby is an absolutist, an all-or-nothing man.[7] At first his employer is greatly pleased with his diligence. "As if long famishing for something to copy, he seemed to gorge himself on my documents." At the last, however, he declines to work at all; with Bartleby there are no half-measures. This absolutism is the mainspring of his character and the cause of his spiritual isolation, his great affliction. His isolation is projected in his quality of neutrality; Bartleby is a total nonconductor, with no relation to his fellow men. "Had there been anything ordinarily human about him, doubtless I should have violently dismissed him from the premises. But as it was, I should have as soon thought of turning my pale plaster-of-paris bust

[7] In this characteristic of the hero, as also in other respects, "Bartleby" is related to Melville's novel, *Pierre*. See Dichmann, "Absolutism in Melville's *Pierre*," *PMLA*, Vol. LXVII (1952), 702-15.

of Cicero out of doors." Again, the narrator is "strangely goaded on to encounter him in new opposition—to elicit some angry spark from him answerable to my own. But, indeed, I might as well have essayed to strike fire with my knuckles against a bit of Windsor soap." This impervious neutrality is ludicrously shown in the circumstance of Bartleby's diet. He apparently subsists on the ginger-nut cookies which the office boy is commissioned to bring to him. Yet Bartleby's food has no influence on his nature. "Now, what was ginger? A hot, spicy thing. Was Bartleby hot and spicy? Not at all. Ginger, then, had no effect upon Bartleby. Probably he preferred it should have none."

Bartleby's constant refrain is, "I would prefer not to," a statement nicely modulated to avoid even the relationship of direct opposition. There is simply no current connecting him to anyone else. This fact is tested: on one occasion the narrator directly challenges him.

"Bartleby," said I, "Ginger Nut is away; just step around to the Post Office, won't you?" (it was but a three minutes' walk) "and see if there is anything for me."
"I would prefer not to."
"You will not?"
"I *prefer* not."

Bartleby is a melancholy Thoreau who has reduced his existence to an ultimate simplicity. Unlike Thoreau, however, he is passive; he has not premeditated and freely willed his isolation. His will is perverted beyond any hope of redemption. His god, the narrator, is genuinely well disposed toward him and offers him a generous number of choices, but he will choose nothing. In fact, although apparently he is freely offered an opportunity to choose, he yet seems predestined not to. When we first meet Bartleby, he has already been wrecked, although we never know quite how. His plight, also, is more immediately social than it is theological or metaphysical. Bartleby has been struck down and then exploited by American society, although again we do not know quite how. In the great competition for success he is one of the losers, one of those who slip uncared-for beneath the waters. "Ah, happiness courts the light, so we deem the world is gay; but misery hides aloof, so we deem that misery there is none." Bartleby is above everything an inoffensive person, an object of compassion.

His employer is at times outraged at the scrivener's refusal to do his work, but Bartleby's resistance is passive only, and he is really powerless in the hands of his society. His peculiarity is his absolutism; he embraces wholly what others make only a part of their lives. Thus he performs the unhappy service of demonstrating the full implications of modern, civilized, commercial life. This intermixture is evident in the main scenes of "Bartleby." The scrivener is a victim of his environment, yet he deliberately brings out the worst in it. His employer, upon taking him into his office, for his own convenience sets off and isolates Bartleby behind "a high green folding screen." After a short period his clerk refuses to emerge from behind it. The narrator is continually conscious "that behind his screen he must be standing in one of those dead-wall reveries of his." And Bartleby's last milieu in The Tombs is a duplicate and ultimate extension of his office.[8] "And so I found him there, standing all alone in the quietest of the yards, his face towards a high wall, while all around, from the narrow slits of the jail windows, I thought I saw peering out upon him the eyes of murderers and thieves." The Tombs is the ultimate prison. "The surrounding walls, of amazing thickness, kept off all sounds behind them. The Egyptian character of the masonry weighed upon me with its gloom."

Bartleby reaches out to embrace, or is utterly mastered by, the most destructive elements in his environment. The narrator finds out accidentally that Bartleby is living in the office. He has no home; he does not go to church; his only connection with humanity is the connection essential if he is to exist at all, his job, and that relation too he severs. Coming upon Bartleby in the office on a Sunday morning, his employer reflects, "What miserable friendlessness and loneliness are here revealed! His poverty is great; but his solitude, how horrible! Think of it. Of a Sunday, Wall Street is deserted as Petra; and every night of every day it is an emptiness." When the lawyer finally moves his business to get rid of Bartleby, the scrivener remains, and there is a kind of indecency in withdrawing the screen of his isolation, as if Bartleby is indissolubly wedded to the ills which have been heaped upon him. "Throughout, the scrivener remained standing behind the screen, which I directed to be moved the last thing. It was withdrawn; and, being folded up like a huge folio, left him the motionless occupant of a naked room."

---

[8] Pierre also ends in The Tombs, after being gradually deprived of all hope.

When the new tenant banishes Bartleby from the office, he haunts the building, "sitting upon the banisters of the stairs by day, and sleeping in the entry by night." He leaves only when the landlord has him arrested and he is taken to The Tombs.

"Bartleby" has been taken to be an allegory of Melville's own situation, and more extensively of the problem of the author in nineteenth-century America. The parallel between Melville's eye trouble and Bartleby's (Pierre also suffers in the same way)[9] has been advanced as evidence for this interpretation, and certainly the occupation of law scrivener or "writer" has its possibilities. Melville's tremendous natural allusiveness of mind, moreover, makes it inherently probable that he was aware of "Bartleby's" personal application, and of the resemblance between "writer" and "author." If, however, these themes represent his main intention in the story, then the worse for Melville. It would make him guilty of a puerile irony and an elaborate trick upon the well-meaning reader, who, I take it, has more in view than Melville's personal troubles. Bartleby as representative man is certainly more interesting than Bartleby as author, or than Bartleby as Melville.

It is not necessary to argue out the case for the univer-

[9] "His incessant application told upon his eyes. They became so affected that some days he wrote with the lids nearly closed, fearful of opening them wide to the light. Through the lashes he peered upon the paper, which so seemed fretted with wires. Sometimes he blindly wrote with his eyes turned away from the paper;—thus unconsciously symbolizing the hostile necessity and distaste, the former whereof made of him this most unwilling states-prisoner of letters" (*Pierre*, Bk. XXV, *iii*).

sality of the story. Two or three points, however, may be made in passing. First, the final sentence of "Bartleby": "Ah, Bartleby! Ah, humanity!" has a very plain significance. It is a universal conclusion. Second, Bartleby's eye-trouble has more implications than merely an autobiographical parallelism. It fits the pattern of intermixed predestination and free will which runs through every situation. "I looked steadfastly at him, and perceived that his eyes looked dull and glazed. Instantly it occurred to me, that his unexampled diligence in copying by his dim window for the first few weeks of his stay with me might have temporarily impaired his vision." The narrator, then, has exploited Bartleby, though perhaps unintentionally; he cannot evade some responsibility for his scrivener's plight. On the other hand, Bartleby's "unexampled diligence" is more than was required of him, and he himself is partly to blame. This semiblindness has another aspect, too. Does it dim Bartleby's spiritual vision, so that henceforth he sees only darkness, as the Minister in Hawthorne's story is confined to darkness by the formidable black veil?

Third, the beginning of the story, which at first appears to be only a conventional frame, has nevertheless universal implications. The narrator has found scriveners "an interesting and somewhat singular set of men." He has known many of them, and "if I pleased, could relate divers histories, at which good-natured gentlemen might smile, and sentimental souls might weep." Of all these Bartleby was the most interesting, and the strangest. Unfortunately no materials exist for a full account of him.

"It is an irreparable loss to literature." Of Bartleby the narrator knows only what he has seen, except for one vague report. The whole passage is a kind of synecdoche, a part which stands for the whole. The quasi-historical purpose of the narrator, although it may be thought only a formal induction like the discovery of the scarlet letter, is likewise a metaphor of a serious pursuit of meaning. The narrator is in his degree a fisher of souls. To Melville one knowledge stands for all knowledge, as the quasi-scientific cetology of *Moby Dick* is in reality a manual of method for investigating spiritual truth. For Scrivener, therefore, read man; and since the narrator is an employer of scriveners, to that degree he is their god and sees them from above. And Bartleby is the strangest, the most insoluble of all his problems.

"Bartleby," as frequently with Melville, is a leisurely and allusive story. The scene is carefully set, the other characters are fully introduced, before Bartleby appears. This leisurely fullness of exposition is in keeping with the quasi-biographical purpose of conveying information about a noteworthy person in an interesting occupation. Once Bartleby is introduced, the story proceeds in a cumulative, slow, remorseless motion towards its inevitable conclusion; the movement is repetitive and gradual. Bartleby is throughout defined primarily by his relations with the narrator, but at first he is placed against the background of the other clerks—the casual and everyday, by which he is implicitly judged. As Bartleby's destiny narrows, however, Turkey and Nippers gradually disappear; the scrivener's spiritual isolation approaches the absolute. The settings work in the same way. Bartleby is symbolically imprisoned in his corner of the office.

I placed his desk close up to a small side-window in that part of the room, a window which had originally afforded a lateral view of certain grimy backyards and bricks, but which, owing to subsequent erections, commanded at present no view at all, though it gave some light. Within three feet of the panes was a wall, and the light came down from far above, between two lofty buildings, as from a very small opening in a dome. Still further to a satisfactory arrangement, I procured a high green folding screen, which might entirely isolate Bartleby from my sight.

Thus the narrator plays the role of fate. He does not, however, deprive Bartleby of his free will; he does not demand or even expect that Bartleby should *live* in his corner. The scrivener himself embraces and enforces his imprisonment. He refuses to leave the office and hovers forlornly on the stairs when he is finally evicted. The final setting of The Tombs, explicitly a prison, is a duplication of the narrator's law chamber. Again, as hitherto, Bartleby insists upon his destiny, refusing all palliation. He could look at the sky, but instead he faces the inner wall. "Bartleby" is a story of absolutism, predestination, and free will, in which predestination undoubtedly predominates. The scrivener has been perverted before the story opens; the narrator-god perhaps unwittingly assists in his undoing; and his later well-intentioned efforts to rescue Bartleby are so futile as to be merely ironic. The slow, regular, repetitive movement of the story is the

heavy tread of "predestinated woe," in a blending of
meaning with structure.[10]

[10] For some previous interpretations of "Bartleby," see Richard
Chase, *Herman Melville* (New York, 1949), 143–49; Arvin, *Herman
Melville*, 242–44; Charles G. Hoffman, "The Shorter Fiction of Herman Melville," *SAQ (South Atlantic Quarterly)*, Vol. LII (1953),
418–21; and Leo Marx, "Melville's Parable of the Walls," *Sewanee
Review*, Vol. LXI (Autumn, 1953), 602–27. Marx's essay is the only
full-scale treatment of the story that I have seen.

III

# *"Cock-a-Doodle-Doo!"*

THE NARRATOR of "Cock-a-Doodle-Doo!," a young farmer, is a generous, hot-headed man, the kind of good fellow praised by Thackeray and Dickens.[1] He is a lover of humanity and a rebel against the machinery of human society and the processes of human law, which fail to answer the needs and feelings of individuals. His attitude is a humorous but rueful defiance.

At the beginning of the story, the world seems dark to him. Both public and private affairs are in a bad way. Everywhere despotism has conquered freedom, the world is full of senseless casualties, and he himself is being pursued by a persistent creditor. Thus he sallies forth one spring morning, too melancholy to sleep. "It was a cool and misty, damp, disagreeable air. The country looked underdone, its raw juices squirting out all round. I buttoned out this squitchy air as well as I could." It is the miserable interim time of the spring thaw, when even the calves turned out to pasture look miserable, "sharp bones sticking out like elbows, all quilted with a strange stuff dried on their flanks like layers of pancakes."

---

[1] George Warrington, for instance, in *Pendennis*. The revolt against mechanism and institutionalism is a more general theme in the Victorian novel than is usually noticed.

Suddenly, however, he hears a cockcrowing, ringing and triumphant. *" 'Glory be to God in the highest!'* It says those very words as plain as ever cock did in this world." He begins to feel "a little in sorts again." The sound is repeated, and with every crow his spirits rise. The landscape is transformed; the damp mists are "soft curls and undulations" glorified by the sun. Earlier the scene had been "a divided empire," disputed by winter and spring; now, unquestionably, "the old grass has to knock under to the new." The narrator goes home in high spirits, drinks a quart of stout, reads *Tristram Shandy,* and ends the morning by throwing his creditor bodily out of the house, an action accompanied by the loud approval of the cock, "such a trumpet-blast of triumph, that my soul fairly snorted in me."

So far excellent, but there are some questions to be answered. Cocks are generally good at dawn, but they have little staying power. Will this rooster be able to keep it up? Does his crow come from mere sophomoric ebullience and ignorance of the world, or is it a considered and trustworthy expression of ripened thought? These points must be tested. Also the narrator would know the source: where is the cock, and who is his owner? The first two problems are quickly solved. The evening crow is louder than the morning; the cock is steadfast. And clearly it "was the crow of a cock who crowed not without advice . . . the crow of a cock who had fought the world and got the better of it." As to the source, it takes a quest of some days to find it out. The crow is universal; it seems to come from everywhere, and besides, the irregularities of the terrain produce strange and confusing echoes.[2] The narrator inquires about, supposing the cock must belong to some wealthy neighbor. At length he is surprised to find that the owner is a pauper named Merrymusk, who lives with his invalid wife and children in a shanty by the railroad track.

This Merrymusk is wed to misfortune, and yet a happy man with a happy family. The marvelous cockcrowing keeps them all in spirits. In the end, the narrator revisits them to find them all dying, worn out by the world but buoyed up still by the great voice of the cock, who seems to crow their souls to heaven. They die, and with one culminating triumphal outcry the cock falls dead as well. The narrator himself buries them and raises over them a stone "with a lusty cock in act of crowing, chiseled on it, with the words beneath:

> *O death, where is thy sting?*
> *O grave, where is thy victory?"*

"Cock-a-Doodle-Doo!" brings together two Melville heroes of different periods, for the narrator is a close relative of the Ishmael of *Moby Dick,* and Merrymusk is the true protagonist of the tales, the sad Benedict who is indissolubly wedded to calamity, the heartaches and the thousand natural shocks that flesh is heir to. Merrymusk is, as it were, the narrator's elder brother. The narrator of the story is an Ishmael, who cannot go to sea.

---

[2] Compare the narrator's difficulty in "The Piazza" in locating a distant house among mountains, or the tortuous climb in both parts of "The Two Temples."

## "COCK-A-DOODLE-DOO!"

Whenever I find myself growing grim about the mouth;
whenever it is a damp, drizzly November in my soul;
whenever I find myself involuntarily pausing before cof-
fin warehouses, and bringing up the rear of every funeral
I meet; and especially whenever my hypoes get such an
upper hand of me, that it requires a strong moral principle to prevent me from deliberately stepping into the
street, and methodically knocking people's hats off—then,
I account it high time to get to sea as soon as I can. This
is my substitute for pistol and ball. (*Moby Dick,* chap. 1.)

So the narrator steps forth one morning, "too full of
hypoes to sleep," into the "misty damp, disagreeable air."
He also is on the verge of "methodically knocking people's hats off." "If they would make me Dictator in North
America a while, I'd string them up! and hang, draw, and
quarter." Then comes to him the crowing of the cock.

The narrator establishes a bond with Merrymusk by
an act of impulsive good will. Outraged at the sight of
him eating a cold and miserable dinner in the snow, the
narrator hales him inside by his fire and forces better
food upon him. This is an acknowledgment of human
brotherhood, which the pauper values at its true worth.
Merrymusk is, to outward appearance, a forlorn outcast.
He is "tall and spare, with a long saddish face." He
wears "a long, gray, shabby coat, and a big battered hat."
Nevertheless he has "somehow a latently joyous eye, which
offered the strangest contrast" to his general air of defeat.
Merrymusk has been a wanderer, a cheerful, thriftless
man, like Ishmael a sailor; from being rootless, however,
he is now a settled family man. Once inconstant, now his
most noticeable trait is steadfastness. The narrator remarks with what steady industry he saws wood in the snow

31

all day to make a bare living. He is determinedly silent, and the narrator is at first inclined to resent it. Yet, on further thought, he changes his mind. "I concluded within myself that this man had experienced hard times; that he had had many sore rubs in the world; that he was of a solemn disposition; that he was of the mind of Solomon;[3] that he lived calmly, decorously, temperately; and though a very poor man, was, nevertheless, a highly respectable one." This is a description of the typical post-Ishmael Melville hero.

The fabulous cock is everything that Merrymusk is not, and thus is his complement and comfort. Merrymusk is silent, the cock overwhelmingly eloquent; Merrymusk is gray and battered, the cock preternaturally splendid. "His colors were red, gold, and white. The red was on his crest alone, which was a mighty and symmetric crest, like unto Hector's helmet, as delineated on antique shields. His plumage was snowy, traced with gold. He walked in front of the shanty, like a peer of the realm . . . .[4] He looked like some oriental king in some magnificent Italian opera." Merrymusk is the common man, the cock the very principle of the outstanding individual. At the end the two become one, as the cock stands amid the dying Merry-

[3] "The sun hides not the ocean, which is the dark side of this earth, and which is two thirds of this earth. So, therefore, that mortal man who hath more of joy than sorrow in him, that mortal man cannot be true—not true, or undeveloped. With books the same. The truest of all men was the Man of Sorrows, and the truest of all books is Solomon's and Ecclesiastes is the fine hammered steel of woe" (*Moby Dick,* chap. 96).

[4] Compare Chaucer's description of the cock in "The Nun's Priest's Tale." Since Chaucer's story is frankly mock-heroic, the resemblance has some point.

musks "like a Spanish grandee." "There was a strange
supernatural look of contrast about him. He irradiated
the shanty; he glorified its meanness. He glorified the battered chest, and tattered gray coat, and the bunged hat."
Likewise, "the pallor of the children was turned to ra-
diance. Their faces shone celestially through grime and
dirt. They seemed children of emperors and kings, dis-
guised." The glory is the reality.

The crow of the cock is, first of all, a paean of Christian
hope. The Merrymusks' epitaph is a quotation from I
Corinthians, and plainly the cock enunciates Beatitudes.
Blessed are the meek, the poor in spirit; blessed are they
that mourn. He propounds the Christian paradox. He is
also a Shelleyan Romantic poet, though I am not aware
that Shelley's poetic imagery at any time envisages roost-
ers. As with the Skylark, all the earth and air with his
voice is loud, and he inundates the heavens with profuse
strains of unpremeditated art. And, in his transforming
power, he is also a Romantic poet, who penetrates beneath the appearance to reality, who finds in the everyday
the unique, whose touch is magic. In his tremendous brag-
gadocio, he is, however, more distinctively Melville himself,[5] and one recalls that his defiance encourages the de-
fiant narrator. He is the poor man's secret comfort, the
indomitable mockery of the democrat. He is Arrowsmith's

5 "And if any of our authors fail, or seem to fail, then . . . let us
clap him on the shoulder, and back him against all Europe for his
second round. The truth is, that in one point of view, this matter
of a national literature has come to such a pass with us, that in
some sense we must turn bullies, else the day is lost, or superiority so
far beyond us, that we can hardly say it will be ours" (Melville,
"Hawthorne and His Mosses").

scorn of men of measured merriment, the assistant professor's revenge upon his dean.[6] He is, indeed, everyman's dream of telling the boss to go to hell.

Of these meanings, the Christian theme is the most explicit. Yet doubt is cast upon it. The style of "Cock-a-Doodle-Doo!" approaches the mock-heroic in its persistent exaggeration. Whether deliberately or from lack of skill, it makes the tale ridiculous. The symbol of the rooster, too, has jarring connotations. One remembers Chaunticleer of "The Nun's Priest's Tale" and his pride that went before a fall. Encouraged by the tremendous cockcrowing, the narrator adds another mortgage to his debts. "Through the imperative intimations of the cock . . . I came to clap the added mortgage on my estate; paid all my debts by fusing them into this one added bond and mortgage."[7] What if his confidence is misplaced? "Never since then," says he, "have I felt the doleful dumps, but under all circumstances crow late and early with a continual crow." If he has paid off the mortgage, though, we hear nothing of it. There is, too, a latent horror in the death scene of the Merrymusks, perhaps from their passivity of utter trust. What if the crowing of the cock is a hellish exultation over the deluded and lost? Against this interpretation would stand the cock's steadfastness and wisdom, which the narrator remarks more than once, and which is akin to the steadfastness of Merrymusk.

Melville was certainly aware of the possibilities which

6 The present writer is not an assistant professor.

7 This gesture suggests the all-or-nothing absolutism of Bartleby, or of the younger Melville himself, or of Ishmael signing on a whaler.

the story presents, but one suspects that he did not fully control them. The choice of the cock as symbol is not happy, nor the state of mind behind the choice. The tremendous bravura of the style might well be intended to solve the difficulty by brazening it out, but it only magnifies it instead. One inclines to think finally that the story means what it says but betrays something else. Intended as a trumpet call of affirmation, it reveals in its dissonances the note of underlying despair.

# IV

# *The Three Diptychs*

i

"THE TWO TEMPLES" are a fashionable New York church and a London theater. The narrator visits each in search of spiritual recruitment and refuge and finds himself, contrary to expectation, decidedly more edified by the latter. The effect of the comparison is to show that the church is very like a playhouse, and the playhouse, on the other hand, is very like a church. The church is lowered by the parallel, for the ceremonies there become play acting; the theater is ennobled, since the play takes on the dimensions of sacred ritual. The narrator is turned from the doors of the church and only gains admission by a subterfuge; he is admitted into the theater by the charitable act of a workman. The point is ironical, by surprise:

I went home to my lonely lodging, and slept not much that night, for thinking of the First Temple and the Second Temple; and how that, a stranger in a strange land, I found sterling charity in the one; and at home, in my own land, was thrust out from the other.

The indictment of the church is explicit. It is form without substance, matter without spirit. It is "marble-buttressed, stained-glassed, spic-and-span"; its warden, who repulses the humble, dust-stained stranger, is "fat-paunched, beadle-faced." The congregation are proud and rich; their very horses have a haughty curve to their necks. " 'Property of those "miserable sinners" inside, I presume,' " reflects the discomfited narrator. The stained-glass windows of the church are a kind of illusion,[1] which baffles and deludes the sight. Stealing within, the narrator mounts to the second floor of the church tower, which is lighted by "three gigantic Gothic windows of richly dyed glass." But he cannot see out. "After all, it was but a gorgeous dungeon." In order to see, he scratches a tiny opening in a great purple star in the center of the middle window. The congregation, too, are glittering and meaningless. Looked at from above, they take on the windows' coloring. "Then down I gazed upon the standing human mass, far, far below, whose heads, gleaming in the many-colored window-stains, showed like beds of spangled pebbles, flashing in a Cuban sun."

The priest is a mere actor, while the actor is almost a priest. The former is "a noble-looking man, with a form like the incomparable Talma's." His movements suggest stage entrances and exits, and even changes of costume, when he reappears with "his white apparel wholly changed for black." He preaches on a text extremely suitable and agreeable to his audience—"Ye are the salt of the earth." The actor, who happens to be the great Macready as Cardinal Richelieu, "looks every inch to be the self-same, stately priest I saw," and the lighting of

[1] Compare the effect of stained glass in the Roman churches of Hawthorne's *The Marble Faun*.

the stage has precisely the same effect as the stained-glass windows. "He too seems lit by Gothic blazonings." There is, however, one important difference. The religious service was play acting to the end, mere empty form, but when the theater curtain falls, "the enraptured thousands sound their responses, deafeningly; unmistakably sincere. Right from the undoubted heart . . . . In earnestness of response, this second temple stands unmatched."

Wonderingly the narrator asks himself, "And hath mere mimicry done this? What is it then to act a part?" Paradoxically, the true ritual has become the false; the mere semblance has become the reality. By juxtaposing the church and the stage, Melville has artfully indicted the church for absolute hypocrisy, has demonstrated that its doings are diametrically opposite to its sayings. He uses his double structure in the service of satiric wit and enhances his effect by the reversal that comes from surprise. The "message" of "The Two Temples," then, is a conventional attack on institutional religion, an immemorial target for satire.

Yet the question, "What is it then to act a part?" reveals a deeper theme, a wider problem of appearance and reality. The nature itself of reality is laid open to doubt, and the narrator's search is for the truth. He seeks also a communion, since in both sketches he is an outcast who wishes to be taken in by his fellows. Melville makes the desire to go to church of a morning, or to while away a lonely evening in a foreign city, the mask of a deeper longing. In "Temple First," he is denied admission, and steals into the church tower; in "Temple Second," being temporarily penniless, he is given a ticket by a kindly workman. In both sketches he ascends, to find the best point of view and the best opportunity of joining his fellowmen. In the church, climbing from level to level shut in by stained glass ("I seemed inside some magic lantern"), he finds at last a little window from which to look down upon the service. The point of view is comprehensive, but it has two disadvantages. The window is a ventilator, and covered by fine wirework,[2] so that there is a film between the narrator and clear reality. Since it is a ventilator, it is also uncomfortably hot, high up as it is in the wall. The building has been constructed for the comfort of the worshippers below, not for the benefit of the outcast gazing down from a peephole. "The furnace which makes the people below there feel so snug and cosy in their padded pews, is to me, who stand here upon the naked[3] gallery, cause of grievous trouble."

The narrator also mounts in "Temple Second," since his ticket is for the cheap seats at the top of the theater. His passage upward reminds him "of my ascent of the Gothic tower on the ocean's far-other side." The ticket taker is "like some saint in a shrine." He reaches the gallery and finds the same "wire-woven gauzy screen" and "hot blast of stifling air" as in the church, though this time the screen is tobacco smoke. As before, he looks far down upon the higher privileged below. This time, however, "I had company. Not of the first circles, and certainly not of the dress-circle; but most acceptable, right

[2] Compare the eye trouble of Bartleby and Pierre. See above, pp. 23–24.
[3] The adjective carries some weight. The unfortunate of these stories are helplessly exposed to vicissitude. See below in "Poor Man's Pudding," pp. 42–43; "The Piazza," pp. 89–90; "The Encantadas." p. 107, 110.

welcome, cheery company, to otherwise uncompanioned me." He has a comforting sense of communion with the respectable poor people around him, and this sense is made an actuality by the gift of a mug of ale from a good-natured ale boy. " 'Well, dad's gone to Yankee-land, a-seekin' of his fortin; so take a penny mug of ale, do, Yankee, for poor dad's sake.' " The symbolic and sacramental nature of the gift is evident from the narrator's answer to the boy's request to "drink to honest dad." " 'With all my heart, you generous boy; here's immortal life to him!' " Its meaning is underlined by the boy's surprise at his unexpected vehemence: "He stared at my strange burst."

ii

Like "The Two Temples," "Poor Man's Pudding and Rich Man's Crumbs" has a point to make, by means of comparison and contrast. Its twin sketches, "Picture First" and "Picture Second," represent first American, then British poverty.[4] The general point is that, whatever the differences of time and place, the misery of poverty is, has always been, and will continue to be, the same everywhere. "Poor Man's Pudding and Rich Man's Crumbs" bids us to look unblinkingly at the visible truth of the matter, which cannot be palliated either by the self-deception of the tender-minded or the tough insensibility which comes by custom.

American poverty, as Melville is seeing it, is forlorn and anomalous. There is no provision for it in American values and assumptions. British poverty, on the other

[4] The three diptychs make some approach to the international theme of Hawthorne and later, Henry James.

hand, is all too thoroughly accepted. The American poor are rural freeholders, the British the fierce outcasts of great cities. There is no remedy for either, since both are hopelessly isolated from the sympathies of the prosperous. In "Picture First" the gentle poet Blandmour has shrouded his eyes in sentimental optimism, so that he fails to perceive the truth. The poor to him are happy primitives, who lead contentedly the simple pastoral life. He praises "poor man's pudding," in which "a substitute for the eggs may be had in a cup of cold rain-water." Snow is "poor man's manure" and also "poor man's eye-water." Blandmour talks, too, of "poor man's plaster . . . , an alleviative and curative, compounded of simple, natural things." The English officials of "Picture Second" are complacently impervious; inured to human misery by long custom, they laud as "a noble charity" the casting to the poor of the miserable remains of an official banquet. The American paupers eat their poor man's pudding in resigned silence; the English fight like wild animals for rich man's crumbs and riot when they are consumed. "It seemed to me as if a sudden impotent fury of fell envy possessed them."

The narrator of the two sketches sees the truth of the matter and refutes Blandmour and the English officials by his ironies, but part of his clear-sightedness lies in his perception of his own helplessness to aid. With the American poor, the Coulters, he partakes of "poor man's pudding." But he does so as visitor and privileged character, and bitter and mouldy he finds their accustomed food. The English Feast of Lazarus[5] he attends as a spectator

5 The story of Lazarus and Dives appears often enough in the

by arrangement with the responsible officials, and he has a guide to take care of him. Despite this help, his clothes are half torn off, and he barely escapes a really nasty situation. But his separate status is emphasized throughout. " 'Mind, Jehu,' " says his guide to his cabdriver, " 'this is a *gentleman* you carry. He is just from the Guildhall Charity, which accounts for his appearance.' "

The American paupers, Coulter the woodcutter and his wife Martha, are miserable Benedicts most sadly wedded to this world. They are self-respecting and self-reliant—" 'Only let the rheumatiz and other sicknesses keep clear of me,' " says Coulter, " 'and I ask no flavors or favors from any' "—but the imagery in which they and their environment are represented connotes helpless subjection. They lie almost wholly open to all the bitter winds of earth. "The house was old, and constitutionally damp. The window-sills had beads of exuded dampness upon them. The shriveled sashes shook in their frames .... The floor of that room was carpetless, as the kitchen's was." Mrs. Coulter is an embodiment of the heart laid bare, a woman with soft, sad blue eyes, who has lost two children and is carrying a third child within her. " 'Still, still does dark grief leak in,' " says she, " 'just like the rain through our roof. I am left so lonesome now; day after day, all the day long, dear William is gone; and all the damp day long grief drizzles and drizzles down on my soul. But I pray God to forgive me for this; and for the rest, manage it as well as I may.' " Her husband has named for her, Martha, the horse he hopes to buy her, but there

---

stories to be worth mentioning. Lazarus is the forlorn Benedict, Dives the happy Bachelor.

is a grimmer joke in this than he has thought of—the willing horse.

The London paupers are as savage as the Americans are gentle; they are a mob, while the Coulters endure their misery alone. "The beings around me roared with famine. For in this mighty London misery but maddens. In the country it softens. As I gazed on the meagre, murderous pack, I thought of the blue eye of the gentle wife of poor Coulter." These beggars are, as it were, licensed outlaws, like devils in Hell; but like devils they are rigorously confined to their own territory. The Coulters' environment suggests privation, bareness, helpless exposure, while the London mob is a turbulent river which yet must flow only within its banks. It gains access to the Guildhall through a narrow passage. "As we drove slow and wedge-like, into the gloomy vault, the howls of the mass reverberated. I seemed seething in the Pit with the Lost." When their pitiful banquet is finished (the time is 1814, and the charity the remains of an official victory celebration), the beggars riot, but even this has been foreseen as inevitable. The Coulters, then, live in a prison of freedom, the mob in a freedom of imprisonment. The isolation of the Americans is less horrifying but, in the end, perhaps even more cruel.

There is a corresponding distinction in the characters of the oppressors. Coulter must hurry through his noon dinner, for his employer, Squire Teamster, "sits in his sitting-room window, looking far out across the fields. His time-piece is true." In Coulter's words, "He's a good enough man. He gives me work. But he's particular." Coulter's dinner is reinforced with the Squire's last year's

43

salt pork, "which he let me have on account." It is so rank that the narrator cannot stomach it. "To tell the truth, it was quite impossible for me (not being ravenous, but only a little hungry at the time) to eat of the latter." Coulter suffers under the indifferent laws of economics, personified by the Squire, who presumably does not see how hopelessly the dice are loaded against his employee. In the trivial fact that Mrs. Coulter makes her husband come home at noon over the fields for a hot dinner is her anxiety that their lives should keep some social warmth and humanity.[6] But the Squire is at hand with his watch.

The enemies of the London poor cut more of a dash, for they are princes and potentates. ". . . where the thronged rabble stood, less than twelve hours before sat His Imperial Majesty, Alexander of Russia; His Royal Majesty, Frederic William, King of Prussia; His Royal Highness, George, Prince Regent of England; His world-renowned Grace, the Duke of Wellington; with a mob of magnificoes." Whereas the Coulters dine on the Squire's last year's pork, the London beggars eat pheasants, pastries, jellies, but with a good portion of them missing. The beggars are served with "the plundered wreck of a pheasant, or the rim of a pastry—like the detached crown of an old hat—the solids and meats stolen out." The charity, perhaps unconsciously, is a refinement of contempt, and is at length perceived as such by its recipients. "In this sudden mood, or whatever mysterious thing it was that now seized them, these Lazaruses seemed ready to spew up in repentant scorn the contumelious crumbs of Dives."

[6] Compare in "Cock-a-Doodle-Doo!" the narrator's generous horror at Merrymusk lunching on cold bread and meat in the snow.

"Poor Man's Pudding and Rich Man's Crumbs" is explicitly a social document addressed to Melville's fellow Americans of the 1850's. It is not, however, in any narrow respect didactic, since it presents no panaceas for poverty and proposes no course of action. More largely, perhaps, it intends to teach several lessons. First, Americans are not to glory overmuch in their society or presume to be horrified at the inequalities of the Old World, since they are harboring abuses as great and more exquisitely painful to the sufferers. Second is the wider teaching of our common humanity; Melville does not permit the prosperous to escape by calling the unfortunate undeserving. As he invariably does, he scarifies all easy and superficial optimism or cant. With the Coulters, however, he barely escapes sentimentality, for he ennobles them. The narrator substitutes his own idealization for Blandmour's idealization of poverty. His treatment of the Coulters verges upon the pathetic. They have an inner strength which sustains them, but it is passive only, and they are destined to defeat. It is, in fact, this sense of inevitability which rescues the story from mere pathos and makes it tragic, with the values of that suffering which for Melville increasingly constituted the only complete and genuine life.

### iii

"The Paradise of Bachelors" is The Temple of London, once the seat of the Knights Templars but now one of the great Inns of Court. Melville's sketch is a genial, rather Irvingesque account of a convivial evening there as the guest of a hospitable templar. It is well calculated to

attract the genteel American reader by its pleasant por-
trait of an older, more picturesque society. As usual with
Melville, however, there is a good deal beneath the surface, which the genteel reader might not bargain for.

The Temple is just such a refuge from roaring London
as that other temple, the theater. It is the fitting home
for bachelors, not married men.

Sick with the din and soiled with the mud of Fleet Street
—where the Benedick tradesmen are hurrying by, with
ledger-lines ruled along their brows, thinking upon rise
of bread and fall of babies—you adroitly turn a mystic
corner—not a street—glide down a dim, monastic way,
flanked by dark, sedate, and solemn piles, and still wend-
ing on, give the whole care-worn world the slip, and, dis-
entangled, stand beneath the quiet cloisters of the Paradise of Bachelors.

Bachelors are men who have mastered life by learning the
secret of living with impunity. More crudely, they know
how to beat the game. The Bachelors of the Temple dwell
secluded and immune in a great city; they have their own
city, "a city with a park to it, and flower-beds, and a
river-side—the Thames flowing by as openly, in one part,
as by Eden's primal garden flowed the mild Euphrates."
The bachelors indeed live in an Eden, untouched by toil
and care.

The Temple's associations recall to Melville the original bachelors, the monk-knights. But the monk is not
properly the bachelor, for he is austere and wedded to a
purpose; and the knight is not the true bachelor either,
since he goes encased and imprisoned in armor, while the

sensible bachelor is free of encumbrances. Melville hints that the nineteenth century has declined in reality as it has gained in convenience, as a sack suit is less glorious, though more comfortable, than armor. The observation by itself is stale, but it is consistent with the theme of the bachelor.

The dinner which the narrator attends in the Temple is a consummate artifice, a ritual of gracious living. "It was the very perfection of quiet absorption of good living, good drinking, good feeling, and good talk." Everything is managed with wonderful skill and decorum. There is abundance without excess, comfort without pretension, pleasure without penalty. Melville is lost in admiration, which expresses itself in a style excited even for him. This is indeed "the very Paradise of Bachelors." This life is the highest art. It is encased in form and pleasant tradition; the bachelors are celibate priests, who perform a delightful ritual.

Here Melville undoubtedly speaks sincerely, and his sketch is a graceful acknowledgment to his actual host, Robert Francis Cook.[7] His good humor is unmistakable. Yet the very exaggeration of his praises implies a criticism. "The thing called pain, the bugbear styled trouble—those two legends seemed preposterous to their bachelor imaginations. How could men of liberal sense, ripe scholarship in the world, and capacious philosophical and convivial understandings—how could they suffer themselves to be imposed upon by such monkish fables? Pain! Trouble! As well talk of Catholic miracles. No such thing." The

[7] See *The Complete Stories of Herman Melville* (ed. by Leyda), 465–66, for the factual background of the sketch.

47

passage is genial, but unquestionably satiric. The bachelor's ritual is a little empty, a form without sufficient substance to maintain it. It is a kind of enchantment, not life itself, and somehow it must end.

"The Tartarus of Maids" recounts a winter visit to a paper factory, which is situated in a mountain valley in Massachusetts. As in the other "diptychs," Melville precisely parallels the situation of its forepiece for comparison and contrast. As the Paradise of the Temple is a refuge, an oasis, a cloister, a South Sea isle of peace in the roaring sea of the soul,[8] so the Devil's Dungeon, which is entered through a pass called the Mad Maid's Bellows-pipe, lies "right out from among bright farms and sunny meadows." The scene has a certain picturesqueness, "a sort of feudal, Rhineland, and Thurmberg look, derived from the pinnacled wildness of the neighboring scenery," which recalls the different picturesqueness of the Temple. As he darts through the Black Notch into the valley, the narrator remembers dashing in a runaway omnibus beneath the arch of "dark and grimy Temple Bar." Within the valley the factory buildings are irregularly grouped and achieve a factitious quaintness from the irregularity of the terrain, although there is really nothing quaint about them. "The long, high-gabled main factory edifice, with a rude tower—for hoisting heavy boxes—at one end, standing among its crowded outbuildings and boarding-houses," resembles "the Temple Church amidst

8 "For as this appalling ocean surrounds the verdant land, so in the soul of man there lies one insular Tahiti, full of peace and joy, but encompassed by all the horrors of the half known life. God keep thee! Push not off from that isle, thou canst never return!" (*Moby Dick*, chap. 58.)

the surrounding offices and dormitories." The narrator reflects that "this is the very counterpart of the Paradise of Bachelors, but snowed upon, and frost-painted to a sepulchre." The difference outweighs the likeness, which exists to accentuate it.

"The Tartarus of Maids" has become mildly celebrated for its amazing sexual imagery, not least from the interesting question of how Melville got away with it in *Harper's Magazine* in 1855. The machines of the paper factory are elaborately equated with sex organs, and the production of paper with gestation. There is no doubt whatever about this interpretation. The papermaking process takes exactly nine minutes, and it commences with "two great round vats, full of a white, wet, woolly-looking stuff, not unlike the albuminous part of an egg, soft-boiled." Further documentation seems needless, but one wishes, of course, to know the purpose of the sexual metaphor.

In this Tartarus of Maids the sex imagery coexists with imagery of Hell. There is the Mad Maid's Bellows-Pipe and The Devil's Dungeon, and the factory machines suggest implements of infernal torture. The employees are all maidens, for married women "are apt to be off-and-on too much. We want none but steady workers." In other words, the workers must live for nothing but the machines they tend; they are the damned at their eternal labors. Hell is a system of perverted values, in which the machines have taken on the vital functions, and the human beings have become their slaves. From another point of view, to these cast-out maidens, the victims of modern society, their sex is a hell, a system of fatal machinery

49

which they helplessly and fruitlessly tend.[9] The proprietor of the factory is "a dark-complexioned, well-wrapped [the thinly clothed girls shiver with cold] personage," a bachelor, whom his employees call Old Bach. He is clearly the Devil, and this title is a partial disguise for Old Scratch. The bitter cold, which is like Dante's ninth circle in *The Inferno*, is also the maids' enforced virginity, and, as in "Poor Man's Pudding," it is the world's general harshness to the unfortunate. The creative process of the machine, however, is carried on in "a strange, blood-like, abdominal heat," stolen, as it were, from its human slaves.

The setting of the hollow is white, the paper mill is white ("like some great whited sepulchre"), and the maids are ghastly white. It is so cold that the cheeks of the narrator freeze in "two white spots like the whites of your eyes." They are treated by rubbing them with snow. As the circulation again begins, "a horrible, tearing pain caught at my reviving cheeks. Two gaunt bloodhounds [note the play on "blood"], one on each side, seemed mumbling them. I seemed Actaeon." Such is the effect of the sight of these pitiful Dianas, the factory maids, upon the sympathetic observer. Within the factory he sees a tall girl "feeding the iron animal with half-quires of rose-hued note-paper which, at every downward dab of the piston-like machine, received in the corner the impress of a wreath of roses. I looked from the rosy paper to the

---

[9] "The evidence which I have presented can lead to no other conclusion than that Melville constructed out of experiences and scenes around Pittsfield a story in which he presents the biological and social burdens of women contrasted to men" (E. H. Eby, "Herman Melville's 'Tartarus of Maids,' " *Modern Language Quarterly*, Vol. I [1940], 100).

pallid cheek, but said nothing." The power for the factory comes from a reddish stream named Blood River, and it strikes the narrator as "strange that red waters should turn out pale chee—paper, I mean." The blood is stolen from the girls, who are drained white. The mechanical has taken on organic life, the organic become mere mechanism.

The narrator's Virgil, who conducts him through the factory, is a small boy named Cupid, "a dimpled, red-cheeked, spirited-looking, forward little fellow, who was rather impudently, I thought, gliding about among the passive-looking girls . . . yet doing nothing in particular that I could see." Love in this case is blind, as always, only in young Cupid the blindness is to human misery, which custom has made commonplace. This boy horrifies the narrator more than anything else he sees. "More tragical and more inscrutably mysterious than any mystic sight, human or machine, throughout the factory, was the strange innocence of cruel-heartedness in this usage-hardened boy." And, as Cupid, the presence itself of the lad is a cruelty. His name makes him the nexus which specifically links the sexual with the sociological theme in "The Tartarus of Maids," although the two are intermingled in the images of the factory.

One striking instance of this fusion is especially worth notice. Cupid leads the narrator

to a great light room, furnished with no visible thing but rude, manger-like receptacles running all round its sides; and up to these mangers, like so many mares haltered to the rack, stood rows of girls. Before each was vertically

51

thrust up a long, glittering scythe, immovably fixed at bottom to the manger-edge. The curve of the scythe . . . made it look exactly like a sword. To and fro, across the sharp edge, the girls forever dragged long strips of rags, washed white, picked from baskets at one side; thus ripping asunder every seam, and converting the tatters almost into lint. The air swam with the fine, poisonous particles, which from all sides darted, subtilely, as motes in sunbeams, into the lungs.

The "swords" are turned outwards, and the narrator reflects that "just so, of old, condemned state-prisoners went from the hall of judgment to their doom: an officer before, bearing a sword, its edge turned outward, in significance of their fatal sentence. So, through consumptive pallors of this blank, raggy life, go these white girls to death. The girls sharpen the blades with whetstones, and are thus their own executioners, "themselves whetting the very blades that slay them." The maids, then, are condemned to consumption from steadily breathing the deadly air, and are forced to assist in their own destruction. It seems reasonable, however, to interpret the swords also as phalli, and to draw another conclusion from the fact that the blades are turned away. This information is given in answer to a seemingly random question of the narrator's immediately after he has asked if the proprietor of the factory is a bachelor; the juxtaposition is probably not accidental.

"The man, then, I saw below is a bachelor, is he?"
"Oh, yes, he's a Bach."
"The edges of those swords, they are turned outward

from the girls, if I see right; but their rags and fingers
fly so, I cannot distinctly see."

"Turned outward."

In any event, the girls get no good of these blades.

The machines have other meanings as well. Melville's
mind is too broadly allusive to be satisfied with a single
metaphor or pattern. Thus the narrator asks whether the
great papermaking machine makes anything but foolscap.
He is answered, " 'Oh, sometimes, but not often, we turn
out finer work—cream-laid and royal sheets, we call them.
But foolscap being in chief demand, we turn out foolscap
most.' " This is a multiple hit at mass production, the
publishing business, and some theories of American de-
mocracy. The narrator, incidentally, is a seedsman, who
has come to purchase envelopes for the distribution of
his seeds. The occupation at once glances at the author's
trade[10] and at the exploited maids, since these sterile girls
must make the containers for his fertile product. Again,
the blank paper which drops from the machine reminds
him of Locke's *tabula rasa* psychology, which "compared
the human mind at birth to a sheet of blank paper; something destined to be scribbled on, but what sort of characters no soul might tell." Finally, and above all, the
great machine is a fearful necessity. "Always, more or less,
machinery of this ponderous, elaborate sort strikes, in
some moods, strange dread into the human heart, as some
living, panting Behemoth might. But what made the
thing I saw so specially terrible was the metallic necessity,
the unbudging fatality which governed it." And in the

10 As does Bartleby's occupation of law scrivener, or "writer."

53

narrator's vision the girls are bound to the machine and move with it helplessly, pallid as the paper it manufactures. "Slowly, mournfully, beseechingly, yet unresistingly they gleamed along, their agony dimly outlined on the imperfect paper, like the print of the tormented face on the handkerchief of St. Veronica." "The Tartarus of Maids" is social protest, but not social protest merely. Under the immediate impact of Melville's imagination, the situation takes on the aspect of fatality, and the maids are humanity enslaved by the all-conquering[11] machine.

[11] For previous interpretations, see Eby, cited above; Chase, *Herman Melville*, 159–63; Arvin, *Herman Melville*, 236–38.

v

# *"The Lightning-Rod Man" and Three Studies in Failure*

i

"The lightning-rod man," like Hawthorne's "Egotism; or, The Bosom Serpent," jumps so fast into allegory that its visual images are ludicrous. Like the actual serpent which so greatly inconveniences Roderick Elliston, the lightning-rod man is so flatly a personification that he is in literal terms absurd. "His singularity impelled a closer scrutiny. A lean, gloomy figure. Hair dark and lank, mattedly streaked over his brow. His sunken pitfalls of eyes were ringed by indigo halos, and played with an innocuous sort of lightning: the gleam without the bolt." Melville is trying to unite an allegorical scheme of meaning with humorous realism of detail, as if Kafka were to have collaborated with, say, Robert Benchley on an off day. The situation is not improved by a style which is at once staccato and apocalyptic. This is the worst one can say of "The Lightning-Rod Man," which is nevertheless lively, entertaining, thoughtful, and mercifully short. The difference between an ordinary failure and one of Melville's is Melville's genius; his intellectual and emotional vitality infuses life into seemingly dead materials, and he makes something of projects he should never have tried.

55

The lightning-rod man is a salesman who makes his calls in stormy weather. He visits the narrator in his mountain home (in the Acroceraunian[1] Hills!) during a thunderstorm. He makes a vigorous attempt to sell his wares, meets with determined sales resistance, attempts to assault the prospect, and is ignominiously flung out of doors. In the meanwhile the two have conducted a heated argument.

The lightning-rod man endeavors to capitalize upon fear, whereas the narrator seeks to preserve an uncommitted freedom of action. To the narrator the mountains are not only the most glorious but the safest place to be in a storm; to the salesman, " 'You mountaineers are most exposed. In mountainous countries the lightning-rod man should have most business.' " The narrator stands firmly on his own hearthstone, which the salesman begs him to quit as dangerous. One must avoid, he says, contact with any object whatever. The safest place is the middle of the room, and the safest room is placed between an attic and a cellar. The best policy, in fact, is to stay as far from danger as possible and to keep far away from anything at all outstanding. Especially one should avoid tall men in a thunderstorm. " 'Are you so grossly ignorant as not to know, that the height of a six-footer is sufficient to discharge an electric cloud upon him?' "

The lightning-rod man is preaching abject submission to external power, itself assumed to be an unmixed evil. He advocates complete self-insulation, or isolation. To

[1] Jay Leyda points out the title of Cotton Mather's *Magnalia Christi Americana*, Bk. VI, chap. III, "Ceraunius. Relating remarkables done by thunder" (*The Complete Stories of Herman Melville*, *xxvii*).

be safe, one must relinquish all associations and all action and cower in solitude. The narrator is to leave his hearth-stone; he must not bar the shutters against the beating rain, for the iron bar is a conductor. He must do penance, endure meaningless discomfort: " 'It is the safest thing you can do . . . to get yourself thoroughly drenched in a thunderstorm; and so, if the lightning strike, it might pass down the wet clothes without touching the body.' " One may succeed in appeasing the powerful, that is, by judicious self-abasement. The logical end of the sales-man's argument would be complete intellectual, moral, and physical paralysis.

At the end, "spite of my treatment, and spite of my dissuasive talk of him to my neighbors, the Lightning-rod man still dwells in the land; still travels in storm-time, and drives a brave trade with the fears of man." He is evidently ineradicable from human society; under favor-able conditions he inevitably recurs. It has been sug-gested that Melville was thinking of a hell-fire preacher, who feeds on the superstitions of the simple-minded, but the lightning-rod man is any conscienceless demagogue who takes advantage of a diseased condition by first play-ing upon the sufferer, then offering a universal panacea far more harmful than the disease itself. The salesman carries with him his lightning-rod, his remedy. The im-plications of his advice are remarkably contemporary; they suggest strongly the dangers of "guilt by association," a doctrine which would end by emphasizing the dangers of association with anything. The meaning of the light-ning-rod man is still more general: he is the personifica-tion of Fear itself, "the dark lightning-king," and he is the envy of the gods, a false Fate which destroys all men who dare to aspire. The narrator mocks at him as "Jupiter Tonans."[2]

Against him the narrator rears a truer Fate, a broader theory of predestination. " 'The hairs of our heads are numbered, and the days of our lives. In thunder as in sunshine, I stand at ease in the hands of my God . . . . See, the scroll of the storm is rolled back; the house is unharmed; and in the blue heavens I read in the rainbow, that the Deity will not, of purpose, make war on man's earth.' " God's purposes are unknown, and creation is both good and evil. The lightning is grand, but the narrator does not deny its powers of destruction. One does not cower, however; one stands up and looks at the visible truth of good and evil alike. In the midst of predestination, the spirit is free.

## ii

"The Happy Failure," "The Fiddler," and "Jimmy Rose" form a natural trio, since they are all studies in the values of failure. In the first, the narrator's uncle is a projector, who has invented "the Great Hydraulic-Hydrostatic Apparatus for draining swamps and marshes." He believes in progress; reminded that a Roman emperor failed to drain the Pontine marsh, he replies proudly that " 'The world has shot ahead the length of its own diameter since then.' " His great machine fails utterly; the uncle, crushed at first, quickly rallies and takes comfort.

---

[2] Richard Chase by implication makes the narrator, Prometheus, "a phallic divinity" and the salesman, Zeus, "everything that inhibits and corrupts the moral, aesthetic, civilizing creativity of sex" (*Herman Melville*, 163).

The moral lesson he draws from his experience is less than electrifying: " 'Boy, take my advice, and never try to invent anything but—happiness.' " His failure, however, has restored his humanity to him,[3] which his machine had nearly destroyed. " 'Praise be to God for the failure'!" There is a hint that the uncle has been saved from a Frankenstein monster or a serpent which would have squeezed out his essential life, in the description of the "Apparatus." "I peeped in, and saw a surprising multiplicity of convoluted metal pipes and syringes of all sorts and varieties, all sizes and calibres, inextricably inter-wreathed together in one gigantic coil. It looked like a huge nest of anacondas and adders." Figuratively, the great coil menaces its own creator.

The uncle is a lesson to his young nephew. "If the event made my uncle a good old man, as he called it, it made me a wise young one. Example did for me the work of experience.' " So Hautboy, the hero of "The Fiddler," is an example to the narrator Helmstone, an aspiring young poet whose poem has miserably failed.[4] Helmstone is introduced by his wise friend Standard to Hautboy, who serves as an instance of human goodness and happiness in adversity. The poet is impressed, but upon reflection denies the relevance of this object lesson. " 'With average abilities; opinions clear, because circumscribed; passions docile, because they are feeble; a temper hilarious, be-

[3] Compare Hawthorne, in whose fiction ambition almost always leads to spiritual isolation.
[4] Compare Hawthorne, "The Devil in Manuscript," *The Snow Image.* The writer, Oberon, burns his manuscripts so enthusiastically that he starts a general conflagration, at which he exults that at last "my brain has set the town on fire!"

cause he was born to it—how can your Hautboy be made a reasonable example to a heady fellow like you, or an ambitious dreamer like me?' " Hautboy has no temptation to be other than he is.

It turns out, though, that Hautboy has earned his happiness to the full. He is a former infant prodigy, a violinist who in his boyhood had achieved the greatest success and celebrity. In his day he "has been an object of wonder to the wisest, been caressed by the loveliest, received the open homage of thousands on thousands of the rabble." Now he makes a poor living by giving lessons from house to house and is "happier than a king." The poet is completely convinced by this dramatic disclosure: "Next day I tore all my manuscripts, bought me a fiddle, and went to take regular lessons of Hautboy." One might ask, of course, of what precisely Helmstone is convinced, and why he must abandon poetry. The imitation seems literal unto slavishness. Furthermore, their situations are not truly parallel. Hautboy has at least had his success, and his happiness rests upon his possession of genius, "*with* genius and *without* fame." Helmstone has had no success, and we are not told the value of his poetry; the story verges upon sentimental cynicism in its assumption that the world never rewards achievement at its true value. This assumption, indeed, is dangerously close to the conclusion that genuine achievement does not exist. The character of Hautboy is interesting, nevertheless, in evoking from Melville a serious statement of the attitude of the mature man: "It was plain that while Hautboy saw the world pretty much as it was, yet he did not theoretically espouse its bright side nor its dark side. Rejecting all solutions, he but acknowledged facts. What was sad in the world he did not superficially gainsay; what was glad in it he did not cynically slur; and all which was to him personally enjoyable, he gratefully took to his heart." Hautboy is Melville's ideal clear-sighted, uncommitted man. "Rejecting all solutions, he but acknowledged facts."

Jimmy Rose, the third failure, is a once prosperous and popular New York merchant who has gone through bankruptcy. His ruin opens his eyes to the sad truth of human nature, for his friends, except one, abandon him. Shocked, he hides like a sick animal and drives away at pistol-point the only man who seeks him out, the narrator of the story.

At this point the narrator loses sight of him for many years. The change in Jimmy Rose is astonishing. "He whom I expected to behold . . . dry, shrunken, meagre, cadaverously fierce with misery and misanthropy—amazement! The old Persian roses bloomed in his cheeks. And yet poor as any rat; . . . a pauper with wealth of polished words; a courteous, smiling, shivering gentleman." Jimmy has taken upon himself a most subtle penance. Recovering himself, he has not retired from the scene of his prosperity but lingered as a guest of the more fortunate, to whose homes he makes regular though tactful visits around teatime, not presuming to dinner. His choice is from his goodness, symbolized by the continuing rose of his complexion; his bloom is never quite rubbed off. "Perhaps at bottom Jimmy was too thoroughly good and kind to be made from any cause a man-hater."

Melville's emphasis is upon Jimmy's goodness and his consequent tragic victory. Part of the ordeal for each of our three failures is the requirement that he should keep before him the circumstances of his defeat and confront them continually. In his first despair the uncle in "The Happy Failure" tries to demolish his invention completely, but, upon consideration, keeps the container for a woodbox and turns over the remains to his black servant to sell as old iron for tobacco money. Hautboy does not abandon his fiddle, but lives by giving lessons on it. So Jimmy Rose returns to his society. With him, however, Melville suggests in his plight a possible refinement of cruelty, which the other two stories do not possess. "Sometimes sweet sense of duty will entice one to bitter doom . . . . Without rudely breaking him right down to it, fate slowly bent him more and more to the lowest deep." Jimmy's roses are, it may be, undying: "Transplanted to another soil, all the unkind past forgot, God grant that Jimmy's roses may immortally survive!" Yet Melville makes us wonder if God has not taken advantage of poor Jimmy's fineness to torture him to the limit, before good-naturedly excusing him for the rest of eternity. The story reminds one a little of the cat-and-mouse ordeal of Hunilla, the Chola widow.[5]

[5] "Dire sight it is to see some silken beast long dally with a golden lizard ere she devour. More terrible, to see how feline Fate will sometimes dally with a human soul, and by a nameless magic make it repulse a sane despair with a hope which is but mad. Unwittingly I imp this cat-like thing, sporting with the heart of him who reads." ("Norfolk Isle and the Chola Widow," in "The Encantadas". See below, pp. 106–109.

# VI

# "The Bell-Tower"

"THE BELL-TOWER" is a Poe-like story of the Italian Renaissance, elaborate and decorative, and with something of
Poe's metallic resonance. It marches, too, toward its conclusion with Poe's remorselessness. It is more leisurely
than Poe, however, and it is genuinely concerned with
ideas as Poe never is. It is a true, not simulated, allegory.
The death of the proud Bannadonna is the victory of the
machine over its human creator. Melville's epigraph
"from a private MS." renders the general meaning of the
story unmistakable:

> Like negroes, these powers own man sullenly;[1]
> mindful of their higher master; while serving,
>            plot revenge.
> The world is apoplectic with high-living of
>     ambition; and apoplexy has its fall.
> Seeking to conquer a larger liberty, man but
>     extends the empire of necessity.

"The Bell-Tower" 's symbolism is rich and complex, but
yet more regular than is usual with Melville, more formal
and more consistent. The tale commences with its ultimate result, the stump and outline of a ruined tower.

[1] Compare the revolt of the Negro slaves in "Benito Cereno."

These are like the stump and the fallen remains of a great pine, and the metaphor is carried on through the bells, an ironic fusion of organic life with mechanical construction. "From that tree-top, what birded chimes of silver throats had rung. A stone pipe; a metallic aviary in its crown: the Bell-Tower, built by the great mechanician,[2] the unblest foundling, Bannadonna." The specification for Bannadonna is significant. It is appropriate that a "mechanician" should possess no organic tradition of continuity, should rise without the sanction of accepted religious belief.

The tower is the product of an age of innovation and human pride, the early Renaissance. It is a second Tower of Babel after the flood of the Dark Ages. "No wonder that, after so long and deep submersion, the jubilant expectation of the race should, as with Noah's sons, soar into Shinar aspiration." Melville displays it rising slowly from the surrounding plain, "snail-like in pace, but torch or rocket in its pride," the builder always "standing alone upon its ever-ascending summit." This tower is man's aspirations to power and freedom through science, it is Bannadonna in his pride, and it is, at least apparently, a vantage point of ever widening vision. From it at last the builder can see "the white summits of blue inland Alps, and whiter crests of bluer Alps off-shore—sights invisible from the plain." But as the view stretches out, one remembers the sentence from Melville's epigraph, "Seek-

2 See Charles A. Fenton. " 'The Bell-Tower': Melville and Technology," *American Literature*, Vol. XXIII (1951), 220. In his article, Mr. Fenton draws detailed parallels between the "Renaissance" of "The Bell-Tower" and the technological development of nineteenth-century America.

ing to conquer a larger liberty, man but extends the empire of necessity." Bannadonna alone dares stand three
hundred feet high on the still-unrailed summit. He has
accustomed himself, however, to heights. "His periodic
standing upon the pile, in each stage of its growth—such
discipline had its last result."

The builder is superhuman in daring and presumption.
His great state bell is too heavy, as the magistrates, who
stand for traditional wisdom, give him warning. In what
seems a suggestive play on words, they caution him that
"though truly the tower was Titanic, yet limit should be
set to the dependent weight of its swaying masses." At
the casting of the bell, "the unleashed metals bayed like
hounds," so that the workmen recoil till Bannadonna
drives them back by striking and killing their chief. "From
the smitten part, a splinter was dashed into the seething
mass, and at once was melted in." This bit of human alloy,
however, leaves a flaw in the casting, though Bannadonna
skillfully conceals it. The machine has a strange life of its
own, and the circumstance of the flaw indicates that
machines cannot be isolated and rationally used as mere
instruments. Man and machine are essentially diverse and
discordant, and yet are fated to mingle in evil union. And
it is possible that in this union the machine will pre-
ponderate.

This mingling continues in the imagery of the bells.
Bannadonna's designs are grandiose and revolutionary.
Round the great clock-bell are twelve dancing girls, hand-
in-hand—"the embodied hours." A quasi-human figure,
the builder's most prized invention, will strike the hours
precisely upon the handclasps. But about these figures,

alike mechanical and human, there is something ominous and troubling from their mixed existence itself. Mechanical perfection is not maintained, for Una, the hour of one, is subtly unlike her sisters. There is a fatality in her smile, which reminds the chief magistrate of Deborah the prophetess. Bannadonna's explanation for this difference is illuminating. There is a law, he says, which prevents the possibility of duplicates. "The variation of less than a hair's breadth in the linear shadings round the mouth" is sufficient to change the expression completely. The mechanician is, however, fatally confusing his genres. The impossibility of duplication, as in the difference-in-likeness of leaves on a tree, is a principle of organicism, and in mechanics an imperfection. In the sequel, one finds that this ambiguous Una represents Bannadonna's own human weakness, which, although it is in its own field a virtue, destroys him when confronted with mechanical accuracy. For Bannadonna dies because he is not only a mechanician but an artist, at the first stroke of the bell. He has wound up his robot to emerge infallibly at one, then hurries to the bell, "to give his final touches to its sculpture. True artist, he here became absorbed . . . ." Oblivious, he is killed by his punctual iron slave, who strikes at the handclasp of Una and Dua and crushes the intervening skull of his creator. There is an added touch in the speculation that at the moment of death Bannadonna was trying to change Una's expression into uniformity, in a still further confusion of human and mechanical value.

The robot itself demands attention. The enduring fascination of the mechanical human being, from the Frankenstein monster to current science fiction, comes from its ambiguity. Is it alive? and with what kind of life? superior or inferior to humanity? Melville's is *sui generis,* not "after the human pattern, nor any animal one . . . , but . . . an original production." Yet it suggests both human being and giant insect, like Kafka's "Metamorphosis" and much science fiction. "It had limbs, and seemed clad in a scaly mail, lustrous as a dragon-beetle's. It was manacled." Thus it is also slave, and it is with manacled hands that Bannadonna is struck down. The builder, we are told, had secretly far more in mind than a mere clock-mechanism. The slave was to be at least an unheard-of mechanical perfection, "a new serf, more useful than the ox, swifter than the dolphin, stronger than the lion, more cunning than the ape, for industry an ant, more fiery than serpents, and yet, in patience, another ass. All excellences of all God-made creatures, which served man, were here to receive advancement, and then to be combined in one." The slave's name is to be Talus, the iron giant.

The robot has also, however, another dimension of meaning. He is the type of the master as well as of the slave. There is a hint of this in the magistrate's warning that the tower may fall from "the dependent weight of its swaying masses." Bannadonna has imagined his figure as not only a slave but an inhuman, iron dictator, the embodiment of power. His original inspiration was the human figure seen from far below, as on the top of a tower: a position in which it seems an impersonal mechanism. "Perched on a great mast or spire, the human figure, viewed from below, undergoes such a reduction in its apparent size, as to obliterate its intelligent features. It evinces no personality." In this other aspect, with grim humor Bannadonna names him "Haman." For the builder, his creation is at once self-glorification and self-satire, and for Melville, a comment on some theories of the great man. For us he may have an even sharper meaning. He is a glance at the conditions of absolute power, where the ruler is a robot to the mass below; or say he is a prophecy of the full development of the machine, in an age where man *can* be wholly enslaved by a dictator who is backed by modern technology and robot-minded technicians.

As a scientist, Bannadonna is a practical materialist. "However marvelous his design, however apparently transcending not alone the bounds of human invention, but those of divine creation, yet the proposed means to be employed were alleged to have been confined within the sober forms of sober reason." He is not, Melville specifies, a magician; he has no metaphysical belief in the correspondence of mechanical forces and animal organic vitality;[3] he does not hope to discover the source of life; he is not an alchemist; he is not a theosophist who imagines that "by faithful adoration of the Highest, unheard-of powers would be vouchsafed to man." He intends in fair fight to rival nature, outstrip her, and rule her; not to form with her an occult alliance, or somehow steal into her secret. "With him, common sense was theurgy; ma-

---

[3] Contrast Hawthorne, "The Artist of the Beautiful," which deals with the same problem of organicism and mechanism. Owen Warland "had considered it possible, in a certain sense, to spiritualize machinery, and to combine with the new species of life and motion thus produced a beauty that should attain to the ideal which Nature has proposed to herself in all her creatures, but has never taken pains to realize." He creates a marvellous butterfly, which "has imbibed a spiritual essence—call it magnetism, or what you will."

chinery, miracle; Prometheus, the heroic name for machinist; man, the true God." He seeks the glorification of man, then, by the rational use of the machine as an instrument, and assumes that man can use machinery without himself being altered or affected by it. As we have seen, however, he dies because this is impossible. His reasoning is again refuted after his death, as the clock-bell, "strangely feeble somewhere at its top," breaks away from its fastening and plunges three hundred feet to the ground. The weak spot is the splinter from the head of the unfortunate workman whom Bannadonna killed. Again the human and the machine are shown to be inextricable. The destruction of the builder's work is completed by nature herself in belated revenge upon her opponent, for on the first anniversary of the completion of the tower it is leveled by an earthquake. "The stone-pine, with its bower of songsters, lay overthrown upon the plain."

Melville concludes "The Bell-Tower" with Poe-like economy and precision, as it were one hammer blow to each nail. "So the blind slave obeyed its blinder lord; but, in obedience, slew him. So the creator was killed by the creature. So the bell was too heavy for the tower. So the bell's main weakness was where man's blood had flawed it. And so pride went before the fall." The story is recognizably of the genre of the supernatural tale of terror, and as such is very skillfully done, although perhaps too heavily ornate and too regularly symmetrical for most modern tastes. But "The Bell-Tower" is especially notable in its harmony of meaning with superficial form. Melville has considerable to say, but he succeeds in saying it without breaking through the rigid limits of his genre. Thus, in

the creation of the robot and his concealment by Bannadonna, Melville makes continuous use of ambiguity for
suggestion and suspense, up to the climax of the revelation
and Bannadonna's death. This ambiguity, familiar in
stories of the supernatural, is a way of eating one's cake
and having it, too—that is, of asserting the marvellous as
impressively as possible while easing it down the reader's
throat by suggesting alternative natural explanations. It
can be a mere clever trick, but it can also be deeply meaningful when the ambiguity is real and important.[4] The
central ambiguity of "The Bell-Tower" is the problem of
the robot's life.

Talus, or Haman, appears at first a veiled statue. "But,
as the object rose, a statuary present observed, or thought
he did, that it was not entirely rigid, but was, in a manner,
pliant." The city magistrates inspect the tower before its
formal opening and are disquieted by a number of circumstances. The cloaked robot seems to change its position, "or else had before been more perplexingly concealed by the violent muffling action of the wind without."
Near the top of the covering cloth the warp has been partially withdrawn, "so as to form a sort of woven grating."
No more is said of this, but one wonders if the robot needs
to breathe. In the corner is an earthen cup, "just such a
one as might, in mockery, be offered to the lips of some
brazen statue, or, perhaps, still worse." The builder explains it matter-of-factly as a cup "to test the condition
of metals in fusion." So uneasy are the magistrates, how-

4 On "ambiguity," see Yvor Winters, *Maule's Curse* (Norfolk,
Conn., 1938), 18; Matthiessen, *American Renaissance*, 276–77; R. H.
Fogle, *Hawthorne's Fiction* (Norman, 1952), 9–13.

ever, that they fear that when they descend the tower, "the mechanician, though without a flesh-and-blood companion, for all that, would not be left alone." Standing on a landing below, they hear what sounds like a footstep, but Bannadonna explains the noise as falling mortar. He is markedly anxious to get them away from the tower.

The chief ambiquity is in the tableau of Bannadonna's death scene. The robot leans over him "like Jael over nailed Sisera in the tent"; its clubbed arms are lifted as though to strike again, and one foot is inserted beneath the dead body, "as if in the act of spurning it." The common-sense explanation is that the body has clogged the mechanism and checked in mid-motion its return to its place after striking the bell. We do not see the magistrate's final action, but are left in the crowd below. A spaniel has followed them up the tower. An arquebus is called for, and there is a shot, "followed by a fierce whiz, as of the sudden snapping of a main-spring, with a steely din, as if a stack of sword-blades should be dashed upon a pavement." The spaniel is seen no more and that night the re-cloaked robot is sunk far out at sea. Has the dog scented some unnatural being, attacked it, and been killed? "It is generally thought that the arquebus was used on the spaniel, gone mad with fear."

The robot is essentially, if not literally alive. Bannadonna may have skillfully played on the magistrates' credulity, or he may have honestly tried to hide something which to them would have seemed impious, although to him it was a mere feat of mechanics. The ambiguity lies between his point of view and theirs; and theirs, if not literally, is essentially the correct conclusion.

71

# VII

# "I and My Chimney" and
# "The Apple-Tree Table"

### i

THE CONSERVATISM of the narrator is a sub theme of "Jimmy Rose." William Ford is an elderly man who lives in an old house inherited from relatives. Jimmy Rose, who once lived in the house, is a treasured memory of the past for him. Thus he is fond of his dwelling for its associations and traditions. His wife ("who, I fear, was too young for me") and his daughters wish to make modern alterations, but he refuses. Especially he refuses to change a gaudy *rose-patterned* wallpaper for the "beautiful, nice, genteel, cream-colored" paper that they desire.

The unnamed narrator of "I and My Chimney" is practically the same man transplanted to the country from New York.

Old myself, I take to oldness in things; for that cause mainly loving old Montaigne, and old cheese, and old wine; and eschewing young people, hot rolls, new books, and early potatoes, and very fond of my old claw-footed chair, and old club-footed Deacon White, my neighbor, and that still nigher old neighbor, my betwisted old grape-vine, that of a summer evening leans in his elbow for cosy company at my window-sill, while, I, within doors, lean over mine to meet his; and above all, high above all, am fond of my high-manteled old chimney.

Like William Ford, he has a wife and two daughters who prefer a little newness in things. His wife in particular, though old as himself, is the very spirit of innovation. "By what perverse magic, I a thousand times think, does such a very autumnal old lady have such a very vernal young soul?" She rises early in the morning, full of new plans; always buys her almanac a month before the new year; "and above all, high above all, would fain persecute, unto death, my high-manteled old chimney." She habitually addresses her husband as "Old man," and is continually trying to take over from him the management of their property.

The narrator's conservatism, symbolized by his chimney, aims at the preservation of organically human values, ties, and relationships. He favors the crooked line of life and nature, as is attested by his affection for his "betwisted old grape-vine." His chimney is too large, too generous for modern living; it takes up too much of the house; it is too rambling and irregular; it is uneconomical in its vast number of bricks, which tie up too much capital. Thus it is seriously threatened, and it is the narrator's chief care to preserve it from the persistent attacks of his family and neighbors. He hardly dares to leave home for fear of what might happen to it in his absence.

Melville treats the chimney as an indivisible, inexhaustible object in itself. That is, many meanings are attached to it, but it is larger than any of them singly and larger than the sum of them. It preserves its own unique identity;

when all has been said, it is simply (or complexly) a chimney still. It has a kind of magic about it, but its enchantment can be finally neither elucidated nor broken. This chimney is perhaps most obviously the life principle of the house as a structure. Like the great chimney of *The House of the Seven Gables,* it is the heart from which life comes, by virtue of which the house is a sentient and even a human entity. Its genial warmth pervades the whole:

At the second landing, midway up the chimney, is a mysterious door, entering to a mysterious closet; and here I keep mysterious cordials, of a choice mysterious flavor, made so by the constant nurturing and subtle ripening of the chimney's gentle heat, distilled through that warm mass of masonry. Better for wines is it than voyages to the Indies, my chimney itself a tropic. A chair by my chimney in a November day is as good for an invalid as a long season spent in Cuba. Often I think how grapes might ripen against my chimney. How my wife's geraniums bud there! Bud in December! . . . Ah, a warm heart has my chimney.

This conception of the chimney relates to the theme of conservatism through the imagery of the heart, for the heart, the seat of feeling, is a great conservative both for good and for evil, and remains unchanging in the march of the restless intellect. Likewise, the story proposes another tenet of conservatism: be wary of tearing down, lest you destroy the life itself. The narrator's wife is eager to do away with the chimney entirely, but the house is built around it and could hardly survive its loss. On one occasion, too, she advocates demolishing its foundation and basing the chimney on the second floor, in order to make room for a grand entrance hall. "The truth is," says the narrator, "women know next to nothing about the realities of architecture." An eager projector, in her grandiose plans she forgets the realities of the situation. "At last, I gently remind her that, little as she might fancy it, the chimney was a fact—a sober, substantial fact, which in all her plannings, it would be well to take into full consideration."[1]

In its largest aspect the chimney is a symbol for universal reality, the scheme of things entire. It is vast, mysterious, and so comprehensive that it can be known only partially; no one sees it as a whole. It is visible on three levels: in the basement as foundation, in the house proper as body, and emerging from the roof as top. On one occasion the narrator digs about the base, in an effort to learn the secret of its origin in the earth which hides it. It is significantly remarked that "I was a little out of my mind, I now think." The enterprise might well be dangerous, as a fundamental self-mutilation. A neighbor's joking suggestion that he is loosening the soil to make it grow also has its point, when we recall that, figuratively, the chimney is alive. The chimney is roughly pyramidal in form, and thus is akin to the great pyramids of Gizeh. "The architect of the chimney must have had the pyramid of Cheops before him." It gains size and dignity from the association, along with a certain slight suggestion that the pyramid, broad at the base and narrowing gradually to a point, is the archetypal form of reality and growth. This, however, is merely hinted at. A

[1] "It was plain that while Hautboy saw the world pretty much as it was, yet did not theoretically espouse its bright side nor its dark side. Rejecting all solutions, he but acknowledged facts" ("The Fiddler").

persistent rumor claims that there is a secret treasure-chamber hidden in the chimney, which is one of the pre-texts advanced for tearing it down. The rumor is, however, untrue, as the narrator steadily maintains. Reality resides in the whole, and in no single part. It might be said that there are no short cuts to knowledge, or, the secret is that there is no secret—none, at any rate, which would warrant the finder in destroying as irrelevant the structure in which it lies embedded.

There is a moral in Melville's chimney for critics and scholars, as for all who pursue knowledge. One might glance at the literary source hunter, who, like the lightning rod man, still operates among us: he who would elucidate his author by means of some hitherto unnoticed source, and thus pluck out the heart of his mystery, whereas his man's identity and power must be in himself alone, whatever he has been able to assimilate into himself.

The search for the treasure, however, has been explained as an ironic reference to Dr. Oliver Wendell Holmes's mental examinations of Melville in 1855.[2] Hiram Scribe, an architect retained to inspect the chimney by the narrator's wife, suspects the presence of a secret chamber in it. The identification sounds probable enough, and would help to explain the architect's invidious name. It would also point to a complex self-irony in Melville, surprisingly jocular and unembittered. If it is true, however, it is also limited in interest, and the moral we have just been rehearsing would warn us not to take it as the "secret" of the story.

Nevertheless, "I and My Chimney" may very well be on

[2] See Merton M. Sealts, "Herman Melville's 'I and My Chimney,' " *American Literature*, Vol. XIII (1941), 142–54.

one plane an allegory of Melville's own condition and circumstances at the time of writing. The identification would explain, for one thing, the emphasis upon the age of the narrator, taken figuratively to apply to the author. As Byron and Shelley had lived many times their years, and died old at thirty-six and twenty-nine, so the volcanic Melville had a sense that he had already outlived his day and that his fires were sinking.[3] By an easy shift the chimney now becomes Melville's writing, his life effort, misunderstood, no longer remunerative, regarded as wasteful and impractical, and, like any genuine thing, disliked and contemned by many. Why not write for the public: tear down the chimney and substitute something more suitable to the time, the place, and the climate?

A little more broadly, the chimney is Melville's genius, or any genius, a possession which may burden even its owner. It is inconvenient to have around the house; it takes up too much space; it interferes with household routine. It is hard upon the genius's family and friends, who must either remove themselves or live in its shadow and accommodate themselves to it. It may be difficult to distinguish from outrageous and willful eccentricity, with

3 "I am like one of those seeds taken out of the Egyptian Pyramids, which, after being three thousand years a seed and nothing but a seed, being planted in English soil, it developed itself, grew to greenness, and then fell to mould. So I. Until I was twenty-five, I had no development at all. From my twenty-fifth year I date my life. Three weeks have scarcely passed, at any time between then and now, that I have not unfolded within myself. But I feel that I am now come to the inmost leaf of the bulb, and that shortly the flower must fall to the mould" (Letter to Hawthorne, June 1 [?], 1851). Note the reference to the Pyramids, since the chimney is pyramidal, and the resemblance of Melville's development to the circumstances of "The Apple-Tree Table," discussed below, pp. 82–83.

which the narrator's wife repeatedly taxes him. It has not been mentioned that the chimney is truncated; a previous owner, replacing the old gable roof with a lower modern one, took off some fifteen feet to keep it in proportion. In the personal allegory with Dr. Holmes's mental examination, this truncation is a piece of broad self-mockery. If the chimney is Melville's career and his genius, it represents a time of cautious retrenchment and retreat, or a compromise with outward circumstances impossible to fight outright. If the chimney is a form of universal reality —and it is—then the truncation is an interesting reflection upon the present state of man's relations with God. The spirit no longer communes with the sky.

The best relation, however, of superficial with underlying meaning, would take it that the genial, conventional conservatism of the old worthy who is the narrator is a veil which part reveals and part conceals a more urgent and fundamental struggle by Melville, who is fighting to preserve what is best in himself and his life's work at a time when it seems to be threatened seriously. The concealment is almost too successful, since the narrator and his wife are comic "humors" characters of a long and moribund tradition. The good nature of "I and My Chimney" is expansive to the point of being tiresome. But the central image itself is subtle, comprehensive, and vigorous.

ii

The characters of "The Apple-Tree Table" are about the same people as the principals of "Jimmy Rose" and "I and My Chimney," although little is said of the age of the husband-narrator. As in "Jimmy Rose," this family of husband, wife, and two daughters, with a comic Irish maid-servant, Biddy, live "in an old-fashioned quarter of one of the oldest towns in America." This atmosphere of eld properly introduces the old apple-tree table that the narrator finds in his garret.

The discovery and subsequent study of the table is a quest for knowledge of the truth, and a study of the various conditions of the search and of their effect upon interpretation. The table is in the garret, which the narrator ignores until he accidentally finds the key to it, "a large and curious key, very old and rusty." He reflects that "the possession of a key to anything at once provokes a desire to unlock and explore; and this, too, from a mere instinct of gratification, irrespective of any particular benefit to accrue." To know, then, once a clue has been given, is a fundamental urge and instinct.

The exploration of the garret is elsewhere discussed in this book and need not be recounted here at length. It is enough to say that it is a study in different planes, perspectives, and lights, like the narrator's climb toward the culminating vision in "The Two Temples." In "The Apple-Tree Table," the final view is a glimpse of immortality, by contrast with the worm-ridden decay of the old garret. "At last, with a sudden jerk, I burst open the scuttle. And ah! what a change. As from the gloom of the grave and the companionship of worms, man shall at last rapturously rise into the living greenness and glory immortal, so, from my cobwebbed old garret, I thrust forth my head into the balmy air . . . ." The passage, as we shall see, is a prefiguration of the story's end.

The table itself is extremely impressive:

When I first saw the table, dingy and dusty, in the furthest corner of the old hopper-shaped garret, and set out with broken, be-crusted, old purple vials and flasks, and a ghostly, dismantled old quarto [Cotton Mather's *Magnalia Christi!*], it seemed just such a necromantic little old table as might have belonged to Friar Bacon. Two plain features it had, significant of conjurations and charms—the circle and tripod; the slab being round, supported by a twisted little pillar, which, about a foot from the bottom, sprawled out into three crooked legs, terminating in three cloven feet. A very satanic-looking little old table, indeed.

It is apparently magical, then, and black magic at that. The narrator's daughter Julia is thoroughly frightened at the apparition of the table on the stairs with "one cobwebbed hoof thrust out." It is a visual illusion, a momentary and accidental distortion, for the narrator is behind it, concealed by the perpendicular slab by which he is carrying it; but the girl sees nothing "but the apparition of the Evil One's foot." This vision colors her subsequent impression of the table.

The apple-tree table, and the manifestation which arises from it, is interpreted in three distinct ways. The two daughters are frankly terrified of it, as is the Irish maid, Biddy. The wife is a determined rationalist, a very Democritus. "True, she could not account for the thing; but she had all confidence that it could be, and would yet be, somehow explained, and that to her entire satisfaction." As for the narrator, he wavers in his attitude between the extreme of Democritus and Cotton Mather.

Examining himself, he finds that by daylight and in company he inclines to be bravely Democritean, but at night, especially when reading the *Magnalia,* he finds much force in Mather's view of things. He is, in fact, while more open-minded than his daughter Julia, like her subject to the power of momentary impressions.[4]

The table, properly refurbished, becomes a breakfast table for the family and a convenient reading table for the narrator. Despite the daughters it is gradually being naturalized into family life, when suddenly and dismayingly it commences to tick. The narrator, by the way, at first has difficulty in locating the sound—another instance of the treacherous variability of impressions. The ticking sound raises this question: "Could Cotton Mather speak true? Were there spirits? And would spirits haunt a tea-table? Would the Evil One dare show his cloven hoof in the bosom of an innocent family?" The narrator is the first to discover the origin of the sound, though the origin is not the explanation. As he watches the table, a small, luminous insect suddenly appears from a crack in it, a "sort of small shining beetle or bug." The ticking "was simply the sound of the gnawing and filing, and tapping of the bug, in eating its way out." He puts a tumbler over it to keep it safe, and the next morning pre-

4 See Frank Davidson, "Melville, Thoreau, and 'The Apple-Tree Table,'" *American Literature,* Vol. XXV (1954), 479–90. Mr. Davidson treats the story as a representation of Melville's religious doubts and dilemmas. He identifies the table with Calvinism, which is at first unacceptable to the narrator's wife and daughters. After it has been varnished, however (a modernized version of the older Calvinism), it is admitted into the family. See also Douglas Sackman, "The Original of Melville's Apple-Tree Table," *American Literature,* Vol. XI (1940), 448–51.

pares to exhibit it triumphantly to his wife and daughters. But it is gone: the maid, coming upon "a 'bomnable bug," has thrown it in the fire and thoroughly rinsed the tumbler. The daughters share her disgust at the notion of a "bug"; their mother, with characteristic practicality, for the time closes the question by cementing the hole.

The ticking, however, after an interval begins again. After an all-night watch by the family, during which the narrator keeps a journal of his impressions, another insect appears. It is so beautiful, "like a fiery opal," that the girls are immediately charmed. "To them, bug had been a word synonymous with hideousness. But this was a seraphical bug; or rather all it had of the bug was the B, for it was beautiful as a butterfly." Thus their earlier false notion is corrected by actual observation of the fact. To elucidate the meaning of this phenomenon, Julia suggests calling in Madame Pazzi, the conjuress, while her tougher-minded mother proposes instead Professor Johnson, the naturalist. The narrator agrees with his wife. " 'Bravo, Mrs. Democritus!' said I, 'Professor Johnson is the man.' "

Summoned, Professor Johnson agrees that the occurrence is wonderful, but he is ready with a matter-of-fact scientific explanation of it.

The wood of the table was apple-tree, a sort of tree much fancied by various insects. The bugs had come from eggs laid inside the bark of the living tree in the orchard. By careful examination of the position of the hole from which the last bug had emerged, in relation to the cortical layers, of the slab, and then allowing for the inch and a half along the grain, ere the bug had eaten its way entirely out, and then computing the whole number of cortical layers in the slab, with a reasonable conjecture for the number cut off from the outside, it appeared that the egg must have been laid in the tree some ninety years, more or less, before the tree could have been felled. But between the felling of the tree and the present time, how long might that be? It was a very old-fashioned table. Allow eighty years for the age of the table, which would make one hundred and fifty years that the bug had lain in the egg. Such, at least, was Professor Johnson's computation.

This, then, is the word of the scientific naturalist. It is respectable, since it gives the facts uncolored by prejudice, emotion, superstition, or mere impression. Plainly, Professor Johnson is more to be regarded than "Madame Pazzi the conjuress." The circle, the tripod, and the cloven hoof of the apple-tree table, like the dark grimness of the lightning-rod salesman, are no more than masks to frighten the naïve and the timorous. Democritus triumphs, and Cotton Mather is banished. Yet the scientific account of the matter is too flat and literal; it is not the meaning itself but a base for the meaning. The narrator's daughter Julia, while giving up her crude notion that the table is activated by malevolent spirits, proposes in its place a refined, modified, and corrected version of the truth.

"Say what you will, if this beauteous creature be not a spirit, it yet teaches a spiritual lesson. For if, after one hundred and fifty years' entombment, a mere insect comes forth at last into light, itself an effulgence, shall there be no glorified resurrection for the spirit of man? . . . I still believe in spirits, only now I believe in them with delight, when before I but thought of them with terror."

As a conclusion, this affirmation is prepared for by the narrator's earlier excursion into immortality, as he burst from the dark garret, "the gloom of the grave and the companionship of worms," into the open air, "the living greenness and glory immortal." Its validity also is rather strengthened than weakened by the "slight sneer" with which the learned professor receives it.[5] It must, I think, be accepted as the explicit meaning of the story. It is, however, enunciated by a naive young girl, and Melville is generally a little chary of entrusting his wisdom to the mouths of babes and sucklings. And the destiny of the insect is a trifle ambiguous. "The mysterious insect did not long enjoy its radiant life; it expired the next day. But my girls have preserved it. Embalmed in a silver vinaigrette, it lies on the little apple-tree table in the pier of the cedar-parlor." There is certainly more faith than proof here. The story is rather an examination of the pursuit of spiritual knowledge than a statement of absolute conclusions, and perhaps the last word lies with the introspective and finally uncommitted narrator. He does not choose to speak it.

[5] "He [Melville] ridiculed, first of all, the apparent esotericism and mysteriousness of science, which he interpreted as pretty largely humbug. He denounced, secondly, the coldness and inhumanity of the scientific mind. Thirdly, he mistrusted the absurd over-confidence of the enthusiasts who thought science would solve every human problem. Fourthly, he saw the analytical methods of the scientists resulting in the destruction of beauty. And he deplored, finally, the struggle between science and religious faith" (Tyrus Hillway, "Melville as Critic of Science," *Modern Language Notes*, Vol. LXV [1950], 411).

# VIII

# "The Piazza"

"THE PIAZZA," last of Melville's short stories, is very close
to fact. It is a sketch, almost a familiar essay, with its scene
in the Berkshires at Melville's farmhouse, "Arrowhead."
The homespun fact, however, is transmuted into symbol.
"The Piazza" concerns vision, perspective, illusion, and
reality. Its surface is archly ornate, self-consciously agreeable, sentimentally fanciful. Its prose is dangerously over-
wrought, with intricate rhythms which nearly become
meters. It is nevertheless a fine piece, with a sustaining
core of intense life, like a fine picture in a fantastically
decorative frame.

"The Piazza," like "Temple Second," seems a study of
stage illusion, or a Lockeian reflection on the doctrine of
secondary attributes, in which the life and color of the
phenomenal world have no real existence but in the eye
of the beholder. The piazza "is my box-royal; and this
amphitheatre, my theatre of San Carlo. Yes, the scenery is
magical—the illusion so complete." Yet finally, perhaps,
the question of reality is left open. "What is it then to act
a part?" demands the narrator of "Temple Second," after
watching Macready play Richelieu. It may be that we
shall never have done with acting on a stage.

Melville seeks the best, the widest, the noblest, the

truest view. Matter-of-factly, "The Piazza" begins with the question where he shall build his porch: north, south, east, or west. He seeks the most beautiful picture, "for what but picture-galleries are the marble halls of these same limestone hills?" Thus, if his view is illusion, it is the illusion of art and beauty. Significantly, he builds his piazza to the north, despite the jeers of his practical neighbors, who point out its exposure to the bitter north wind. "Wants, of winter midnights, to watch the Aurora Borealis, I suppose; hope he's laid in good store of Polar muffs and mittens." There is another aspect to this question, however. "But March don't last forever; patience, and August comes," when the piazza will be pleasantly cool. Also Melville rather courts the exposure to the elements, as somehow more real and fundamental, just as he prefers the dangerous ocean to the safe, dull land, and as, in his writing, Cape Horn bulks large. "But, even in December, this northern piazza does not repel—nipping cold and gusty though it be, and the north wind, like any miller, bolting by the snow, in finest flour—for then, once more, with frosted beard, I pace the sleety deck, weathering Cape Horn." The mountain prospect, too, is like the sea. "The vastness and the lonesomeness are so oceanic, and the silence and the sameness, too, that the first peep of a strange house, rising beyond the trees, is for all the world like spying, on the Barbary coast, an unknown sail." Most important, the north view fronts on Mount Greylock, the noblest object in the surrounding landscape. South, east, and west all have their attractions, softer perhaps and more amenable than the bold northern mountain; but Melville will have the best.

The wide prospect of mountains from this northerly piazza is a symbol of reality, as it is channeled and objectified by visual imagination. Melville has chosen his point of vantage, from where his world can best be seen in all aspects and seasons. It is a shifting, mobile world, changing endlessly with the seasons, with cloud shadows, with variable lights. The mountains, too, are baffling of themselves. The smallest change in point of view will alter their relationships. "These mountains, somehow, they play at hide-and-seek, and all before one's eyes." One object, the single visible house like "an unknown sail" on the Barbary Coast, finally fixes the watcher's attention as he narrows and focuses his vision. This, too, is variable and uncertain: "so situated as to be only visible, and then but vaguely, under certain witching conditions of light and shadow." It is discovered in an unusual light at an unusual angle, the sun dully peering through the haze of forest fires, and otherwise might never have been glimpsed. Thus much for the mode most favorable to discovery.

When first seen, the object is like "one small, round strawberry mole upon the wan cheek of Northwestern hills." A good deal later it is the end of the rainbow on a showery May day. "Fairies there, thought I; remembering that rainbows bring out the blooms, and that, if one can but get to the rainbow's end, his fortune is made in a bag of gold. Yon rainbow's end, would I were there, thought I." It is an object of Romantic longing and nostalgia: the blue flower, the land of heart's desire, A. E. Housman's land of lost content. The knowledge sought, then, is not a "knowledge without desire." Melville is not, however, satisfied with the glamorous suggestions of distance. A few days farther on, "a golden sparkle" defines the object as a cottage, since the glitter must come from glass; it is not, as a matter-of-fact neighbor had suggested, an abandoned barn. Still later, "a broader gleam, as of a silver buckler," must come from a newly shingled roof, and indicates that the cottage has but recently been occupied.

Here the narrator is forced for a time to break off. He is ill and confined to a "chamber which did not face those hills." Convalescent, and in a morbidly sensitive frame of mind, he is painfully afflicted by a tiny but meaningful disaster. "I could not bear to look upon a Chinese creeper of my adoption, and which, to my delight, climbing a post of the piazza, had burst out in starry bloom, but now, if you removed the leaves a little, showed millions of strange, cankerous worms, which, feeding upon those blossoms, so shared their blessed hue, as to make it unblessed evermore—worms, whose germs had doubtless lurked in the very bulb which, so hopefully, I had planted."[1] "O Rose, thou art sick!" Evil lies at the heart of existence and cannot be distinguished from blessedness. Instinctively trying to redress the balance, he suddenly catches sight of the mountain cottage, "dazzling like a deep-sea dolphin," and resolves to seek it out.

The way is complicated, and Melville manages to make it seem a long journey, a quest, a pilgrim's progress. He alludes to Spenser and to Don Quixote. It is an enchanted progress, with overtones of *Midsummer Night's Dream* and a hint that Titania dwells in the cottage. His range

[1] Compare the white roses in the garden of Hawthorne's *The House of the Seven Gables.*

of allusiveness is perhaps excessive, as he also proposes Una and her lamb and a Tahiti girl first catching sight of Captain Cook. The atmosphere is artificial pastoral, with enameled flowers and golden flights of birds, and a ram he meets is "a wigged old Aries" who leads him "along a milky-way of white-weed, past dim-clustering Pleiades and Hyades." The decoration is certainly over-lavish. The journey is nevertheless real, with movement, variation, and a sense of difficulty. Beneath the frosting of pastoral, too, is solid observation of New England coun-try-side. The narrator gains the mountain's base, then takes a dark road, "which, however dark, led up"—a winter wood road. Passing an orchard, he tastes a red apple, tempting as Eve's; but it tastes of the ground. "Fairyland not yet, thought I." The last of the way is path-less, where "none might go but by himself, and only go by daring."

The goal is finally gained, and in the cottage is indeed a lone girl. She is not, though, the fairy queen Titania; her name is Marianna: "Mariana in the moated grange."[2] She and her brother are orphans, who, with no other resource, have housed themselves in an abandoned cottage. Like Coulter in "Poor Man's Pudding," the brother is away all day at hard labor for a bare living. He cuts wood and burns coal, and staggers home at night to fall almost im-mediately in bed. "The bench, the bed, the grave," this is his lot. His sister at home is as isolated as Robert Frost's Hill Wife, who one day steps behind a tree and vanishes forever. Like Mrs. Coulter, she keeps her lonely house and sees no one. All day she sits at her window and sews, her

2 Tennyson's Mariana, no doubt, as well as Shakespeare's.

only company a company of shadows, as the sun moves and the clouds pass overhead. Her lot is as remote and strange as Elaine's in her tower, but she is a poor everyday sufferer ground down by poverty and adversity, like Mrs. Coulter or Hunilla, the Chola widow.

She lives amid prosaic discomfort. The sun, which gilds her cottage like a fairy palace, half burns and nearly blinds her at her sewing; it stirs up the flies and wasps, "such flies and wasps as only lone mountain houses know." It fades her curtain; it scorches and then rots the roof. Everything disillusions: the mountain cottage, enchanting in the distance and to the imagination free from natural ills, is in reality of all dwellings most pitiably exposed to harm.[3] "A mountain house. In winter no fox could den in it. That chimney-place has been blocked up with snow, just like a hollow stump." Like Tennyson's Mariana, the girl is surpassingly weary; she sleeps little and thinks too much, "a wheel I cannot stop." But she has a fancy that she might be cured. Across the valley lies a house on a hillside, a marble house, beautiful and magical. " 'Oh, if I could but once get to yonder house, and but look upon whoever the happy being is that lives there!' " It is the narrator's house, glorified by distance. "The mirage haze made it appear less a farm-house than King Charming's palace." A foolish wish, she says, born no doubt of loneliness and ignorance. But the narrator answers her with weighty gravity: " 'I, too, know nothing; and, therefore, cannot answer; but, for your sake, Mari-

---

3 " 'You mountaineers are most exposed. In mountainous countries the lightning-rod man should have most business' " ("The Lightning-Rod Man").

anna, well could wish that I were that happy one of the happy house you dream you see; for then you would behold him now, and, as you say, this weariness might leave you.' " Marianna is not Titania, and no more is the narrator "King Charming."

He stays henceforth on the piazza, accepting the view from thence as magical illusion. Seeing the far-off golden window, "how far from me the weary face behind it." Yet "every night, when the curtain falls, truth comes in with darkness. No light shows from the mountain."

The simplest interpretation of "The Piazza" would resemble the simplest interpretation of "The Apple-Tree Table." Illusion must yield to hard fact, fancy to observation. This solution, however, is a little flat; it does injustice to the story. The deeper answer is properly no answer at all, but a profession of enlightened ignorance, Montaigne's *"Que sais-je?"* The narrator says, " 'I, too, know nothing; and therefore cannot answer.' " He speaks advisedly for Melville. Truth may break in with darkness, when no light shines from the mountain, but all day the narrator sits in the light, with his broad view before his eyes. Is darkness an aid to seeing? Is the worm in the flowering creeper the only truth? The imagery of the mountains, infinitely various in its potential relationships, seems to tell us that one vision need not disquality another; and perhaps it says also that the comprehensive view is the best. The northern prospect, after all, was carefully chosen.

# IX

# *"The Encantadas"*

MELVILLE'S "THE ENCANTADAS" presents a special problem in literary unity. It has been generally accepted as fine work, and it presents a single image, a unified experience; but as a collection of ten apparently loosely related sketches, it is simply not the sort of thing we are used to appraising.[1] Its immediate purpose is the purpose of many travel books: to interest its audience by exhibiting the exotic and the strange; and for this end the geographical unity of the locality in question is usually considered sufficient. "The Encantadas," however, is a travel book *plus,* in which the Galápagos Islands have been re-created in Melville's imagination and assimilated into his total vision of reality.

The sketches are bound together by two related meanings, the one abstract and explicit, the other, which grows out of the first, concrete and indirect. First, Melville presents a thesis: The Encantadas, barren and blasted by fire, prove by their existence the Fall of Man and of the

[1] Charles G. Hoffman, however, in "The Shorter Fiction of Herman Melville," comments briefly upon the nature of the unity of "The Encantadas": "Each sketch is a narrative unit, but its connection with the other sketches is not merely one of location. Each contributes to the final effect of the whole" (*SAQ,* Vol. LII [1953], 422. See also 423).

world. They look "much as the world at large might, after a penal conflagration. . . . In no world but a fallen one could such lands exist." The islands are also, however, a microcosm of complex reality, viewed by Melville with a creative skepticism akin to Keats's "negative capability," which is willing to say only that the world is more complicated as well as later than you think. These sketches, like the cetology chapters of *Moby Dick* and much else of Melville, are experiments in total, indivisible knowing, imaginative, metaphysical, and scientific. And since they pursue knowledge, they are tentative and cautious; they will not go beyond their data, as for Keats, "Truth is not truth until it is proved upon our pulses."

As an exercise in the methodology of knowledge, "The Encantadas" moves steadily from general to particular. The sketches are strongly visual; indeed, Melville consistently makes use of seeing as a physical symbol for knowing. He first presents the islands to the imagination as a whole, and then proceeds to amplify, analyze, and criticize. In the first two sketches, "The Isles at Large" and "Two Sides to a Tortoise," we perceive the group as one; in the third and fourth, we mount the towering Rock Rodondo to place them in perspective, to see them as they are in themselves and also in their relation to the wide waters around them. Then we enter from the west through the island of Narborough, which stands like a key in the door of Albemarle, largest of the group. Beyond Albemarle are the remaining twenty-three islands, some of them invisible from the Rodondo rock. This latter specification, one presumes, is important. No point of view is literally complete, and the eye has its limitations, which must be reinforced by inference and imagination. At the end of vision is indeterminacy, as the horizon fades; also the most perfect strategy cannot arrange affairs so well that all relevant objects will be simultaneously visible. Sketch Fifth tells how the frigate *Essex* was nearly wrecked on Rodondo in 1813. Sketch Sixth, "Barrington Isle and the Buccaneers," is an agreeable rest in the general movement. The next three sketches are stories of outcasts, associated with particular islands, and the final Sketch Tenth is a summary of these stories, called "Runaways, Castaways, Solitaries, Grave-Stones, Etc." It concludes appropriately with an epitaph inscribed on the grave of a castaway sailor.

The Encantadas prove the reality of evil. (Melville's manner of "proof," it goes without saying, is imaginative rather than logical.) These islands are utterly accursed; they are the forlorn wreckage of some mighty wrath. Like the landscape of Browning's "Childe Roland to the Dark Tower Came," they are horrifying without being impressive. To get an idea of them, says Melville, "Take five-and-twenty heaps of cinders dumped here and there in an outside city lot; imagine some of them magnified into mountains, and the vacant lot the sea." They fail to suggest a purpose and an organization, even an evil purpose. One finds, however, that this is not the whole story. The Encantadas are stripped of all dignity and meaning that they may be reinvested in the inhuman dignity of desolation. They are a hell, inhabited solely by the damned, to whom alone they present attractions. Their lord, however, is not Satan, the figure of eternal defiance, but the huge Galápagos tortoise, the emblem of eternal, hopeless endurance.

In the opening sketches, Melville works as in the *Moby Dick* chapter on "The Whiteness of the Whale" to define the essential evil and quality. The horror of whiteness resides in its ambiguity, for white is all colors and no color at once. The horror of the Encantadas is comprised in their quality of absoluteness, which is like the whiteness of the whale.[2] They are utterly isolated; they are without change. "The special curse, as one may call it, of the Encantadas, that which exalts them in isolation above Idumea and the Pole, is, that to them change never comes; neither the change of seasons nor of sorrows. Cut by the Equator, they know not autumn, and they know not spring; while already reduced to the lees of fire, ruin itself can work little more upon them." Upon these islands rain never falls, yet they are generally weighed down by heavy gray cloud. Equatorial, changeless, rainless, ruined, the Encantadas are absolute in desolation. Their likeness to Hell is emphasized by an allusion to Lazarus and Dives: " 'Have mercy upon me,' the wailing spirit of the Encantadas seems to cry, 'and send Lazarus that he may dip the tip of his finger in water and cool my tongue, for I am tormented in this flame.' " Reptilian life predominates on the Encantadas, while "on most of the isles where vegetation is found at all, it is more ungrateful than the blankness of Atacama." The Encantadas' isolation is enchanced by the helpless passivity with which they lie open to the ills which are heaped on them, as is true of the isolation of Melville's Bartleby the Scrivener.

2 "The islands will drive any man who lives there to the greatest feats of human endurance or to the lowest depths of human depravity" (Chase, *Herman Melville*, 211).

He is a total nonconductor to whom relationships have become impossible; he rejects life. And so it is with the Enchanted Islands. "The chief sound of life here is a hiss." The malevolence of this voice is equaled by its powerless despair; the serpent goes abased on its belly.

Melville's stark picture of desolation is softened, however, by a number of qualifications. Some of these are inevitable in any imaginative writing, while others are peculiar to Melville. An imaginative definition differs from a logical definition of a concept or thing, in that what is defined partakes by association of the elements used to define it. Thus Keats in the shadowy forest of the nightingale cannot see what flowers are at his feet, while yet white hawthorn and the pastoral eglantine, the grass, the thicket, and the fruit tree wild are an integral part of the experience he describes. So Melville lends dignity to the Encantadas by framing them in what they cannot be, because it is in some way better: "old cities by piecemeal tumbling to their ruin," the Dead Sea, the great forests of the North, the Greenland ice fields, "the clear air of a fine Polar day." All these, from human associations or because they have the possibility of change, possess their attractions, of which the Encantadas illogically partake.

These islands arouse Melville despite their unimpressiveness. Extremes and absolutes fascinate him. The Enchanted Isles possess the charm of the unknown, the temptations of danger. Their atmosphere of woe has its own dignity, from their very hopelessness of change or betterment. The barren islands have, in fact, their own pathos and beauty, as Melville found these qualities also in *Clarel* in the hideous blasted deserts of Palestine. The

Encantadas are dignified by the ultimate realities of the sea which imprisons them, where nothing false can survive, where all action is emergency.

This island group is a microcosm of reality, since Melville's imagination struggles to set all entities in a framework of total relationship. The Encantadas are a symbol for the world, as is the *Pequod* of *Moby Dick,* or the frigate *Neversink* of *White-Jacket,* or the river boat of *The Confidence-Man.* A microcosm, however, is not a macrocosm. (I should apologize for the perhaps excessive truth of this sage saying, but in practice the two are often confused.) It has potentially the same attributes, but in a different arrangement and with a different emphasis, and, as a part, it is by definition limited to a single aspect of the whole which it evokes. The aspect of the Enchanted Islands is what they suggest to imagination: they are not literally the world, but a part of the world: their few human inhabitants are not literally mankind, although they stand for mankind, but a particular kind of men.

To Melville reality is one, indivisible, and complex. He accepts its unity as an unchallengeable first premise. Reality is indivisible in that no single element of it can be extricated from its relationships and used to explain the whole. Melville's urge to *know* has the chastening effect of making him tentative and reluctant to draw conclusions. As an aspect of reality, the Encantadas are predominantly dark, but, as a microcosm, they contain potentially all possibilities. Even this island hell has its bright side, if you look for it. The huge Galápagos tortoise is the living proof:

Even the tortoise, dark and melancholy as it is up the back, still possesses a bright side; its calipee or breast-plate being sometimes of a faint yellowish or golden tinge. Moreover, everyone knows that tortoises as well as turtles are of such a make, that even if you but put them on their backs you thereby expose their bright sides without the possibility of their recovering themselves, and turning into view the other. But after you have done this, and because you have done this, you should not swear that the tortoise has no dark side. Enjoy the bright, keep it turned up perpetually if you can, but be honest, and don't deny the black . . . . The tortoise is both black and bright.

"The tortoise is both black and bright," but one notes the entertaining implication that the bright side is not the right side; to see it, you have to turn your tortoise upside down, and to maintain it, you must keep him upside down. If you wish to find brightness on the Encantadas, in fact, you must take unusual measures. At any rate, the black and the bright are both organic parts of the same creature and cannot be separated.

Melville again and again pays tribute to complexity during these sketches. The final truth is hard to fix. Thus, as a trivial instance, reverence for the giant tortoise is no bar to eating him: after a wild nightmare in which three tortoises appear as world-bearing Hindu gods, "next evening, strange to say, I sat down with my shipmates, and made a merry repast from tortoise steaks and tortoise stews; and supper over, out knife, and helped convert the three mighty concave shells into three fanciful soup-tureens, and polished the three flat yellowish calipees into three gorgeous salvers." Such is the complexity and "the hidden cannibalism of things."

The name itself of the Encantadas has a dual significance which corresponds to the ambiguities of Melville's
attitude toward them. Matter-of-factly, discrepancies in
the reckonings of early navigators and baffling winds and
currents actually made them difficult to find, and there
was long a notion that two groups of islands existed. "And
this apparent fleetingness and unreality of the locality of
the isles was most probably one reason for the Spaniards
calling them the Encantada, or Enchanted Group." The
name, however, has another application, which is emphasized by the Spenserian headpieces prefixed to each sketch.
"The modern voyager," it is said, "will be inclined to
fancy that the bestowal of this name might have in part
originated in that air of spell-bound desertness which so
significantly invests the isles." They are wrapped in a
spell of changeless hopelessness, to which Spenser's "en-
chantments drear" are highly appropriate. Yet for Melville the searcher for knowledge the first meaning of Encantada is no less painful; the wavering uncertainties of
the Enchanted Islands are not the least of their evils. Hawthorne's prophecy that he would "never rest until he gets
hold of a definite belief" was accurate and penetrating.
"It is strange," continued Hawthorne, "how he persists—
and has persisted ever since I knew him, and probably
long before—in wandering to-and-fro over these deserts,
as dismal and monotonous as the sand hills amid which
we were sitting. He can neither believe, nor be comfortable in his unbelief; and he is too honest and courageous
not to try to do one or the other."[3] This is the dilemma

[3] Nathaniel Hawthorne, *The English Notebooks* (ed. by Randall
Stewart) (New York, 1941), 432–33.

of the honest seeker when the knowledge he seeks is limitless.

Melville does not cultivate ambiguities for amusement. Some problems can be solved. The Encantadas are hard to find and fix, but men have done so. At a distance the great Rock Rodondo takes on a protean variety of shapes, but on closer approach one perceives its real nature.

It is visible at the distance of thirty miles, and, fully participating in that enchantment which pervades the group, when first seen afar invariably is mistaken for a sail. Four leagues away, of a golden, hazy noon, it seems some Spanish Admiral's ship, stacked up with glittering canvas. Sail ho! Sail ho! Sail ho! from all three masts. But coming night, the enchanted frigate is transformed apace into a craggy keep.

So, too, in *Moby Dick,* the white mass of the murdered whale is likely at a distance to be taken by some timid mariner for shoals or breakers and even charted as such. Melville's comment on the latter passage is very interesting:

And for years afterwards, perhaps, ships shun the place; leaping over it as silly sheep leap over a vacuum, because their leader originally leaped there when a stick was held. There's your law of precedents; there's your utility of traditions; there's the story of your obstinate survival of old beliefs never bottomed on the earth, and now not even hovering in the air! There's orthodoxy.[4]

This is a homily on the topic of the "visible truth": believe only what you see with your own eyes. Perhaps Mel-

4 Chap. 69, "The Funeral."

ville's difficulty and some of his greatness comes, however, from his desire to *know* also the invisible truth, and his refusal to take it on faith or from report.

The great tortoise is the true symbol and protagonist of the islands, and even their deity. The tortoise becomes a myth, in a dream in which the narrator identifies him with the great tortoise of the Hindus, who bears the world upon his back—an apt image for eternal endurance. The size of these creatures, their immense longevity, their sullen perseverance—all these make them symbols and interpreters of the islands' soul. Their heavy armor is a mark at once of strength and of endless alienation. They are above all massive and weighty, yet always tragic and condemned. They are "black as widower's weeds, heavy as chests of plate, with vast shells medallioned and orbed like shields, and dented and blistered like shields that have breasted a battle, shaggy, too, here and there, with dark green moss, and slimy with the spray of the sea." The terrain of the Encantadas is treacherous with clefts and fissures, and the tortoises bear "the ancient scars of bruises received in many a sullen fall among the marly mountains of the isle." These tortoises are noble, pitiable, and wryly comical as well. The narrator tells how, taken on board ship, one giant spent the night trying to walk through the foremast, with an obstinacy which is attributed to "some penal, or malignant, or perhaps a downright diabolical enchanter." "Their crowning curse," it is remarked, "is their drudging impulse to straightforwardness in a belittered world."

The world is a complicated and a dangerous place, and it is well not to be too simple and trusting; it is well to be wary of jumping at conclusions—or bait. The fish around the Rodondo rock are examples of foolish incaution; they jump at any line. "No sooner did the hook touch the sea, than a hundred infatuates contended for the honor of capture. Poor fish of Rodondo! in your victimized confidence, you are of the number of those who inconsiderately trust, while they do not understand, human nature." Likewise, in "Benito Cereno," the good-natured Captain Delano is delighted with the Negro slaves: "There's naked nature, now, pure tenderness and love, thought Captain Delano, well-pleased." The slaves have much to recommend them, but they have recently massacred their white masters in a rebellion which Delano is certainly not socially advanced enough to have approved. To return to our tortoises, their plight in these islands is analogous to man's lot in his world—well meaning, awkwardly valiant, and fated. Their disposition, then, at the hands of the sailors, gives food for uncheerful thought.

"To go up into a high stone tower," begins Sketch Third, "is not only a very fine thing in itself, but the very best mode of gaining a comprehensive view of the region round about." This tower, the Rock Rodondo, is indeed a very fine thing, for in itself it is a state and a hierarchy of the wild sea birds, and obliquely a study of fundamental structure. I am concerned with it here, however, solely as a vantage point used to view the Encantadas amidst their watery environment. "Southwest from our tower lies all Polynesia, hundreds of leagues away; but straight west, on the precise line of his parallel, no land rises till your keel is beached upon the Kingsmills, a nice little sail of, say 5,000 miles." The vision circles full, and is supplemented by imagination. "Yonder, to the East, some six hundred miles, lies the continent; this rock being just about on the parallel of Quito." These immensities serve to place the Enchanted Islands in perspective; there are other lands in the world. "Of the unnumbered Polynesian chains to the westward, not one partakes of the qualities of the Encantadas or Galápagos." On the beaches of these wrecked islands lie "here and there decayed bits of sugar-cane, bamboos, and cocoanuts, washed upon this other and darker world from the charming palm isles to the westward and southward; all the way from Paradise to Tartarus; while mixed with the relics of distant beauty you will sometimes see fragments of charred wood and moldering ribs of wrecks." Now, having, as Melville says, "fixed our relative place upon the sea," we advance upon the Encantadas themselves.

At this point the sketches particularize. They move, focus, concentrate, and move again, in a comprehensive pattern of physical relationships. As was previously suggested, not all the islands are visible from the Rodondo rock. No point of view will include the whole, but the unseen is inferred in imagination from the seen. Narborough is the key and sets the keynote, for it "lies in the black jaws of Albemarle like a wolf's red tongue in his open mouth." Desolate Albemarle has a combined population of 11,000,000 lizards, snakes, and spiders, "exclusive of an incomputable host of fiends, ant-eaters, man-haters, and salamanders." Again, if the instance is not ridiculous, the seen implicates the unseen, and number evokes the uncountable. This is Hell and its population;

Narborough is an active volcano, where "toil the demons of fire."

To the south lie islands once frequented by the West Indian buccaneers. These are a rest or a retarding point in the tragedy of the Encantadas, useful for contrast; they are the bright exception which proves the gloomy rule, and they are the element of variety in Melville's pattern of complexity. The pirates' islands are less desolate than the others; they are supplied with anchorage, water, food, and even grass and trees. Seats carved from stone attest to the fact that the fierce buccaneers had their softer and more sociable moments. Yet on the beaches are remnants of old cutlasses and daggers and fragments of broken jars. "These were signs of the murderer and robber; the reveler likewise had left his trace." This contradictory evidence furnishes a text for a discourse on the complexity of things, the difficulties that lie in wait for single, decisive conclusions:

With a rusty dagger-fragment in one hand, and a bit of wine-jar in another, I sat me down on the ruinous green sofa I have spoken of, and bethought me long and deeply of these same Buccaneers. Could it be possible, that they robbed and murdered one day, reveled the next, and rested themselves by turning meditative philosophers, rural poets, and seat-builders on the third? Not very improbable, after all. For consider the vacillations of a man. Still, strange as it may seem, I must also abide by the more charitable thought; namely, that among these adventurers were some gentlemanly, companionable souls, capable of genuine tranquillity and virtue.

One apparently trivial circumstance takes on enhanced

significance when it is placed against the larger background of Melville's shorter fictions. Although the pirates stayed for months at a time, they never built dwellings, they were never without their ships, and they presumably slept on board and not ashore. They did not, in fact, submit themselves to the influence of the islands; they were never really subjected to the evil enchantment. It was within their power to take what they wanted and reject the rest of the Encantadas. They skated successfully on the thin ice and never crashed through into the deep waters beneath. Thus these buccaneers were, in Melville's scheme of being, *bachelors*.

Melville's characterization presents a tragic dilemma, for his characters are either bachelors, uncommitted men who do not in the deep sense live at all, or benedicts who are wedded to calamity and find life's burden almost intolerable. Captain Delano, the lawyer-narrator of "Bartleby," and the owner of the paper factory in "The Tartarus of Maids" are in Melville's sense bachelors, while Bartleby and Benito Cereno are benedicts, sad married men. The pirates are the only bachelors of the Encantadas. Those who are really committed to the islands are the outcasts, the forlorn of this world, who come here as a last resort, with approximately the same considerations as prompted Satan to live in Hell. They are a various crew: hopeful adventurers, deserting and marooned sailors, detestable misanthropes, and even a few innocent strugglers for happiness and daily bread. But they have one common characteristic. One and all, they stagger beneath an almost unbearable weight; one and all, like the great tortoise, they bear visibly the wounds of the Encantadas.

Southwest of the pirates' islands is Charles's Isle, where lived the dog-king, the subject of Sketch Seventh. This ruler, a brave Cuban adventurer, like Satan found it better to rule in Hell than serve in Heaven. He set out from Peru to build his kingdom with some eighty men and women, whom he held in subjection by "a disciplined cavalry company of large grim dogs," a subversion of natural order which is ominous from the beginning. He was at length deposed; his people proved ungovernable and forced him into banishment, after a bloody pitched battle with his canine army. Then they set up a republic, which they recruited with deserters from passing ships. The result was "a permanent *Riotocracy,* which gloried in having no law but lawlessness . . . . It became Anathema —a sea Alsatia—the unassailed lurking place of all sorts of desperadoes, who in the name of liberty did just what they pleased." No true society or order can flourish on the Encantadas, which are blasted by the primal curse. Taken as a study in government, the moral of "Charles's Isle and the Dog-King" resembles the saying that politics is the science of the possible. The dog-king was blind to the visible truth, the inescapable fact. To people Hell, you need devils, and those who were not before may well become devils in a hellish environment. Given on the one hand the Encantadas and on the other the sort of folk who find it desirable to resort there, the conclusion is certain. The first premise of the Fall is irreversible, and hope shatters itself upon unscalable barriers.

Far to the northeast is the lone island of Norfolk, which calls to mind the story of the Chola widow. This tale, the most fully developed narrative of "The Encantadas," contains some of what is probably the best writing in the series and more of what is undoubtedly the worst. Again and again Melville falls unforgivably into blank verse, as in "where rested now in lasting uncomplaint . . . / he whom untranquil seas had overthrown," or "More terrible, to see how feline Fate / will sometimes dally with a human soul." The Chola woman, her husband, and her brother are put ashore by a French whaler upon Norfolk to hunt tortoises for tortoise oil. The whaling captain contracts to return for them at the end of a four months' cruise. They make a prosperous beginning, but in only a few weeks the two men die before Hunilla's eyes in a boating accident, of which she helplessly watches every detail, like a spectator at a play. At first overwhelmed with grief, after a long interval she revives enough to look for the returning ship, which never comes.[5] She now undergoes a long torture of hope, symbolized by the notches she makes on a bamboo cane, a notch a day. But, as her eventual rescuers notice, after 180 days the notches cease; time has run out for the Chola widow. Questioned, she reluctantly tells why, although Melville only hints the reason, on the grounds that "in nature, as in law, it may be libelous to speak some truths." Evidently men have come to the island, but only to outrage and then abandon her anew. She is at last rescued by the narrator's whaler, which sights her signal handkerchief by accident when the ship is already drawing away from the land.

The innocent Hunilla is one of the islands' devoted unfortunates, wedded and widowed. Like the noble tortoise,

[5] The captain of the whaler is "a merry man," a bachelor, like the pirates.

she endures all ills. Her story ends with the famous sentence, "The last seen of lone Hunilla she was passing into Payta town, riding upon a small gray ass; and before her on the ass's shoulders, she eyed the jointed workings of the beast's armorial cross." Hunilla, the ass, the great tortoise, and the Encantadas, all are martyrs to existence.[6] The Encantadas, however, are evil and piteous alike, whereas there is no evil in Hunilla.

With the story of the Chola widow one is forced to face the issue, who or what is the god of the Encantadas? Who blasted them, who made Hunilla suffer? Melville will not allow us to escape from this question of questions, nor, conscientious in the method of knowledge, will he answer it. This story deals with effects, not causes; yet it will not let causes wholly alone. Ultimate purposes remain inscrutable; yet whatever governs is so indifferent to human values that its actions appear like exquisite cruelty. Why, since we are created, are we not the children of God? "Ah, Heaven, when man thus keeps his faith, wilt Thou be faithless who created the faithful one? But they cannot break faith who never plighted it." Thus

[6] To Richard Chase, the strength of Hunilla is a kind of existentialism. "Putting her 'trust' in the single fact of existence itself, she endured. It was possible to undercut all questions of reality and appearance, desire and knowledge; it was possible to live below them" *(Herman Melville,* 211). F. O. Matthiessen is more optimistic, in an interpretation which is a characteristic of the late 1930's as Chase's is of the late 1940's: "As Melville celebrates her courage, 'nature's pride subduing nature's torture,' he accepts what had been impossible for him when writing *Pierre:* that good can come out of evil, as well as evil from good. He rises to his equivalent for Whitman's affirmation" *(American Renaissance,* 493). For R. E. Watters, Hunilla represents Melville's version of Hawthorne's isolation theme ("Melville's 'Isolatoes,'" *PMLA* Vol. LX [1945], 1139 n.).

very different conclusions can be drawn. "Norfolk Isle and the Chola Widow" is a tale of pathos, the chief device of which is suspense from repeatedly thwarted hope. Its effect is organically related to its meaning, which, however, can turn in two directions. First, man is a noble creature, who by virtue of his humanity is morally superior to his creator. "Humanity, thou strong thing, I worshipped thee, not in the laureled victor, but in this vanquished one." On the other hand, "they cannot break faith who never plighted it." Man suffers from the tragic delusion that he has a contract with God, but the understanding is on his side only. These two meanings are one, however, in their effect. Whether from purpose or mere discrepancy of natures, the result is cruel. "Dire sight it is to see some silken beast long dally with a golden lizard ere she devour. More terrible, to see how feline Fate will some times dally with a human soul, and by a nameless magic make it repulse a sane despair with a hope which is but mad. Unwittingly I imp this cat-like thing, sporting with the heart of him who reads; for if he feel not he reads in vain."

This final sentence gives a clue to the artistic wrongness of "Norfolk Isle and the Chola Widow." Melville did not let it speak for itself. With congenial material which obviously aroused his imagination, he botched the job from overanxiety to do it full justice. Perhaps he wrote too hastily; at all events he gave free rein to his fatal facility with rhetoric and emphasis. The story's defects are not wholly separable from its merits, for its elaborate cadences and uninhibited poetic diction are sometimes deeply moving. Too often, however, the style is a bastard mixture of prose and poetry, and in the telling of the narrative Melville behaves himself like the writer of a Restoration heroic play, who has substituted the effect of admiration for Aristotle's fear. He exhibits his heroine tableau-like, in set poses for our wonder, and even supplies the attitude of the audience. "Nor did ever any wife of the most famous admiral, in her husband's barge, receive more silent reverence of respect than poor Hunilla from this boat's crew." This is certainly the short way, and not the good way, of creating a tragedy-queen.

Upon Hood's Isle once lived the evil hermit Oberlus, the subject of Sketch Ninth. Oberlus is the fullest human embodiment of the Encantadas, more representative than Hunilla in his dual character of misery and wickedness. He is at once pitiable and evil. The cruel rocks, the impenetrable thickets, the treacherous chasms, the unquiet, dangerous seas are the misfortunes, but also the iniquities, of the islands. Like Oberlus, a detestable, subhuman, misanthropic tyrant who lures castaway seamen into slavery, they are alike oppressors and oppressed. Oberlus is the Encantadas at their darkest and worst. Like them, he is the victim of enchantment: "His appearance, from all accounts, was that of the victim of some malignant sorceress; he seemed to have drunk of Circe's cup." Like them, he lies helplessly open to measureless ills; he has been wracked by mighty and merciless powers. "He looked, they say, as a heaped drift of withered leaves, torn from autumn trees, and so left in some hidden nook by the whirling halt for an instant of a fierce night-wind. . . . He struck strangers much as if he were a volcanic creature thrown up by the same convulsion which exploded into sight the isle." Like the Encantadas, he is stunted and twisted by pitiless pressure. "So warped and crooked was his strange nature, that the very handle of his hoe seemed gradually to have shrunk and twisted in his grasp, being a wretched bent stick, elbowed more like a savage's war-sickle than a civilized hoe-handle." Oberlus lives by selling vegetables to passing ships, but no genuine crop will grow upon these blasted islands: he succeeds only in raising "a sort of degenerate potatoes and pumpkins."

Still, however, like the islands, Oberlus is a malevolent enchanter himself. He is like the physician Chillingworth gathering simples (both have a debt to Spenser), except that he is also ludicrous: "When planting, his whole aspect and all his gestures were so malevolently and uselessly sinister and secret, that he seemed rather in act of dropping poison into wells than potatoes into soil." As enchanter, he turns his subjects into beasts. "These wretches were now become wholly corrupted to his hands. He used them as creatures of an inferior race; in short, he gaffles his four animals, and makes murderers of them." His near identity with his island is accentuated by his intimacy with it, for he is acquainted with all its secret places, where he is accustomed at need to take refuge. "Oberlus makes his escape into the mountains, and conceals himself there in impenetrable recesses, only known to himself, till the ship sails." This intimacy, together with his absolute alienation from society, is forcefully conveyed in the circumstance that for fear of his slaves he takes refuge every night in the mountains, "there to secrete himself till dawn in some sulphurous pitfall."

Oberlus is, then, alike wretched and evil. His character-

111

istic secrecy partakes of both qualities; on the one hand, it is a kind of forlorn shame, a natural decorum of hiding ugliness away; on the other, it is sheer hatred of all relationship. "It was his mysterious custom upon a first encounter with a stranger ever to present his back; possibly, because that was his better side, since it revealed the least." Thus the Encantadas seek to cover themselves with "tangled thickets of wiry bushes, without fruit and without a name, springing up among deep fissures of calcined rock, and treacherously masking them." One remembers the ambiguous blankness of the sperm whale, who has no face, and that impressive phrase "the mystery of iniquity." Oberlus is like Jackson, the evil sailor of *Redburn,* who terrorizes yet harrows the heart of the young hero, and the monstrous Claggart of "Billy Budd," who represents "an evil according to nature." With both of these we feel a certain sympathy, for their wickedness is a sorrowful thing. And Oberlus makes his bid for sympathy in a remarkable letter of self-justification left behind him on the island, which is significantly signed, "Fatherless Oberlus." He too asks the question of the Enchanted Islands, why, if God is our creator, is he not our father as well? Oberlus' tone, however, is not the general tone of these sketches; it is broadly and bitterly ironic. The letter has a mocking postscript: "P. S.—Behind the clinkers, nigh the oven, you will find the old fowl. Do not kill it; be patient; I will leave it setting; if it shall have any chicks, I hereby bequeath them to you, whoever you may be. But don't count your chicks before they are hatched." Upon which the text comments, "The fowl proved a starveling rooster, reduced to a sitting posture by sheer debility." This postscript, like the fate of the dog-king, is a lesson in the visible truth, the inescapable fact. The point is this, one supposes: when a starving rooster produces chicks, then expect that good will come from evil; then hope for the redemption of the blasted and accursed Encantadas, victims and instruments of the wrath of an inscrutable deity. The end of Oberlus proves there is no escape, for him no more than for the islands. Fleeing to Payta in Peru, he is thrown into jail on suspicion and general principles:

The jails in most South American towns are generally of the least wholesome sort. Built of huge cakes of sunburnt brick, and containing but one room, without windows or yard, and but one door heavily grated with wooden bars, they present both within and without the grimmest aspect. As public edifices they conspicuously stand upon the hot and dusty Plaza, offering to view, through the gratings, their villainous and hopeless inmates, burrowing in all sorts of tragic squalor. And here, for a long time, Oberlus was seen.

Here misery and wickedness are mercilessly exposed, as the Encantadas lie open "like split Syrian gourds left withering in the sun." For Oberlus, there is finally no place to hide.

The final Sketch Tenth, "Runaways, Castaways, Solitaries, Grave-Stones, Etc.," rounds out the pattern of organization. It returns to the islands as a whole and summarizes their human associations, which are symbolized by physical relics of human occupation. Here and there are the remnants of hermitages and rude stone basins painfully hollowed from the rocks to catch the dew. "Probably few parts of earth have, in modern times, sheltered so many solitaries. The reason is, that these isles are situated in a distant sea, and the vessels which occasionally visit them are mostly all whalers, or ships bound on dreary and protracted voyages, exempting them in a good degree from both the oversight and the memory of human law." These relics, then, correspond with the hellish and absolute isolation of the Encantadas. Since the islands are not only a place but a world, however, the men who have resorted here were at once unified and various in character and motivation. Isolation has brought them all, but some were deserters, some were lost while tortoise-hunting in the dense and breathless thickets inland, and some were pitilessly marooned. Some were daring and seized their fate by the throat; some passively endured. Being a world and a society, the Encantadas have a post office, but in its implications it is surpassingly forlorn. The post office is a bottle staked out on a beach, a device used by the Nantucket whalers to deposit information for passing fishermen. But it often happens that years go by and no one appears. "The stake rots and falls, presenting no very exhilarating object." As a world, the Encantadas are also a graveyard, not only for their inhabitants but for passing ships, who use them as a potter's field. On this note of death the work ends.

The unity of these sketches is comprised in their master theme of the Fall, which is explicitly stated, and in their indirect assertion of the fact of complexity, which is richly documented in their detail. The world is one, and all is relationship, but the relationship is too vast and too difficult for the eye to unravel it. These themes control the method of organization, which uses seeing as a concrete metaphor for knowing. Much can be seen and known and much can be inferred, but not everything. The most perfect human perspective cannot attain to full unity of vision. Some islands remain invisible, and there is always the infinitely fading horizon.

"The Encantadas" is an impressive work, various, profound, and alive. It is infused with the vitality of a genuinely tragic dilemma. Melville, like his admired Montaigne, is a conscientious skeptic, but unlike Montaigne he is unable to accept his own skepticism; he goes on trying to comprehend a world which in his own terms is ultimately incomprehensible. Human meaning and justice evidently do not correspond with the First Principle of being; yet Melville cannot abandon a human partisanship. He cannot, in my opinion, be said to have had a "quarrel with God," for their relation had too much dignity for the term to be appropriate. His tone is not quarrelsome; it has a tragic depth which subsumes his abundant humor and irony. Yet his attitude is not resignation, either. At the last, like the tortoise-god of the Encantadas, it signifies simply endurance.

X

# *"Benito Cereno"*

WITH THE REVIVAL of Melville, "Benito Cereno" was placed very high. To Edward O'Brien it was "the noblest short story in American literature,"[1] to John Freeman, "a flaming instance of the author's pure genius."[2] In the opinion of Carl Van Doren, "it equals the best of Conrad in the weight of its drama and the skill of its unfolding."[3] These are judgments of the 1920's; fuller criticism was delayed until the forties. The two full analyses of "Benito Cereno," by Rosalie Feltenstein and by Stanley T. Williams, agree with the earlier verdict; both are tributes to Melville's artistry. Miss Feltenstein demonstrates "the architectural skill with which the story is constructed," declaring that "there is not one careless, useless, weak, or redundant touch in the whole tale."[4] Professor Williams goes as far, or farther: "Only now are we beginning to realize the perfection of its form and the subtleties of its insights. It is even defensible to prefer 'Benito Cereno' to 'Moby Dick' and 'Billy Budd.' "[5]

[1] "The Fifteen Finest Short Stories," *Forum,* Vol. LXXIX (1928), 909.

[2] *Herman Melville* (New York, 1926), 61.

[3] "A Note of Confession," *Nation,* Vol. CXXVII (December 5, 1928), 622.

[4] "Melville's 'Benito Cereno,' " *American Literature,* Vol. XIX (November, 1947), 246.

On the other hand, two of Melville's best critics have raised important objections. Although F. O. Matthiessen found the story "one of Melville's most sensitively poised pieces of writing,"[6] he could not accept its symbolism, which "was unfortunate in raising unanswered questions."[7] Still more recently, Newton Arvin has rejected "Benito" completely. Its materials are unassimilated, its symbolism labored, its diction trite, its climax thrown away, its meaning trivial and obvious. It is, in short, vastly overrated.[8]

How can one explain this wide divergence in intelligent opinions? The answer is the difficulty of the problems which the story raises. Melville drew it directly from a source, Captain Delano's *Voyages*,[9] and there is room for argument about his use of his source. He stays close enough to make "Benito Cereno" unusually detailed and documentary in its treatment of fact, and it is unquestionably slow-moving. Much of its concluding part is taken up with a court deposition, almost literally transcribed, so that it would be reasonable to judge with Arvin that the material has not been worked up into art. The work is too long for a short story and too short for a novel. Finally, the themes and the meaning of "Benito Cereno"

---

[5] "'Follow Your Leader':—Melville's 'Benito Cereno,'" *Virginia Quarterly Review*, Vol. XXIII (Winter, 1947), 61.

[6] *American Renaissance*, 373.

[7] *Ibid.*, 508.

[8] *Herman Melville*, 238–40.

[9] This fact was revealed in Harold H. Scudder's article, "Melville's *Benito Cereno* and Captain Delano's *Voyages*," *PMLA*, Vol. XLII (June, 1928), 502–32. See also Explanatory Notes, *Piazza Tales*, ed. by Egbert S. Oliver (New York, 1948), 230–34.

are complex, and their proper relationships and ultimate unity are matters not easily settled.

In August, 1799, the American sealer *Bachelor's Delight,* commanded by Captain Amasa Delano, is lying in the harbor of an uninhabited island off the coast of Chili. On the second day of her stay she sights an approaching ship, which appears to be in difficulties. The good-natured Delano decides to board the stranger to steer her to anchorage and give whatever assistance is necessary. Viewed more closely, she proves to be the *San Dominick,* a huge old Spanish merchantman carrying a cargo of Negro slaves.

Aboard the *San Dominick* Delano finds a strange situation. Battered by storms off Cape Horn, long delayed by calms and contrary winds, she has lost by gales, fever, and scurvy the majority of her crew, all her passengers, and many of the slaves. The whites, however, seem to have suffered disproportionately. After this long ordeal, and with almost no officers, there is naturally little discipline left aboard the *San Dominick.* The black slaves swarm about the deck unhindered, and all is noisy confusion. Two particulars especially strike Delano's eye. Four elderly Negroes are so stationed above the crowd on deck as to hint that they exercise some power of control. On the poop sit six Ashantis, busied at polishing the rusty hatchets which are stacked about them. More casually, Delano notices that the ship's figurehead is covered as if for repairs.

Benito Cereno, captain of the *San Dominick,* is a young Spanish gentleman. He is dressed with singular and rather inappropriate richness but is sickly and bowed down by his misfortunes. His conduct is so strange that it suggests madness. Cereno is closely attended by a Negro servant, Babo, with whose fidelity Delano is greatly impressed.

Delano stays on board the *San Dominick* from early morning till six o'clock at night, when she is finally brought to anchor. The interval is caused by a prevailing calm, with contrary currents and tides. During this tedious period Delano is gradually oppressed by some mystery in the situation, with Benito Cereno apparently its center. All is nightmarish and unreal. Cereno is alternately despotic and overindulgent toward his underlings; toward Delano he is successively friendly, fawning, and insultingly indifferent. The slaves, in the main docile, have sudden fits of violence. Several of the Spanish sailors seem to be trying to communicate with Delano but do not make themselves clear. Atufal, a giant black in chains to which Cereno carries the key, keeps turning up suspiciously in inconvenient places. Watching Babo shave the Spanish captain, Delano suddenly fancies that he is seeing a man in the hands of his executioner.

At length the *San Dominick* reaches anchorage, and Delano leaves the ship. Cereno suddenly leaps overside into his boat as his men commence to pull away. Immediately three Spanish sailors fling themselves into the sea, and the servant Babo jumps after Cereno into the American boat, with drawn dagger. For a moment Delano supposes that the Spaniard is pretending to be kidnaped, but he is suddenly enlightened by a cry from one of his boat's crew. Babo is trying to kill his master, not defend him. The slaves are in full revolt, and Babo is their leader. He is overpowered; the insurgent slaves are recaptured, not without casualties; and most of the remaining Spaniards are saved. After some days the *San Dominick* and the *Bachelor's Delight* set sail together for Lima, to put the case before the viceregal courts.

At the trial Cereno reveals the true story of the *San Dominick*. The slaves had revolted, seized the ship, and put to death all of the passengers and many of the crew. Cereno was kept alive to navigate the vessel to Senegal. When she encountered the *Bachelor's Delight,* she was trying to take on water before making the passage to Africa. The servant Babo was the brains of the revolt, the giant Atufal his lieutenant. Delano was left unharmed on the *San Dominick* because Babo planned to take his ship in a surprise night attack and wished to deceive the Americans completely.

Cereno at first promises to regain his health, but then relapses. His spirit has been broken by the malignant Babo. After the trial he retires to a monastery, where he dies in three months' time, thus following Babo, whose eyes look toward Cereno's monastery, his head upon a stake in a public square of Lima.

The primary theme of "Benito Cereno," determined by Melville's emphasis, is Delano's struggle to comprehend the action. The first part of the story is told entirely from his point of view. Later the emphasis shifts partly to the trial, where the causes of the action are revealed. At the end two conclusions are made about the meaning of the facts: first, that reality is a mystery and hard to read, and, second, that evil is real and must be reckoned with. To which should perhaps be added, there are some evils that are cureless and some mysteries insoluble to man. These propositions are related, for the mystery of "Benito Cereno" is a mystery of evil, contrived by an evil will:

"You were with me all day [says Cereno]; stood with me, sat with me, talked with me, looked at me, ate with me, drank with me; and yet, your last act was to clutch for a monster, not only an innocent man, but the most pitiable of all men. To such a degree may malign machinations and deceptions impose. So far may even the best man err, in judging the conduct of one with the recesses of whose condition he is not acquainted. But you were forced to it; and you were in time undeceived. Would that, in both respects, it was so ever, and with all men."

But Delano is not wholly undeceived. And his speech hints at a corollary: once evil has occurred, it is hard to distinguish between its consequences in the perpetrator and in the victim. So, on the deck of the *San Dominick* Delano comes upon a Spanish sailor, with "a face which would have been a very fine one but for its haggardness. Whether this haggardness had aught to do with criminality, could not be determined; since, as intense heat and cold, though unlike, produce like sensations, so innocence and guilt, when, through casual association with mental pain, stamping any visible impress, use one seal— a hacked one."

Delano, the observer of the action, lacks the sense of evil. Without this key he cannot penetrate the meaning until Cereno forces it upon him, and its deeper implications are permanently closed to him. Consequently, the primary theme opposes the appearance, which Delano sees, to the reality, which Delano does not see. "Benito Cereno" is a story of delusion, of a mind wandering in a maze, struggling but failing to find the essential clue.[10] This theme requires that the reader possess the clue withheld from the character, but the final solution must be no more than generally suggested. The reader takes pleasure in his clear superiority to the baffled character, but he must not take the character for a fool. He must sufficiently participate in the bafflement himself to feel suspense. For this purpose ambiguity is useful: a sense of alternative or multiple interpretations and possibilities, keeping us in indecision. Melville makes full use of ambiguity in "Benito Cereno." Finally, both inward and outward action must have, in addition to complexity, development and firm design. The maze must have a structure.

The structure of Delano's experience aboard the *San Dominick* is most simply projected in the unities of time, place, and action. The time is twelve hours, the place is the ship, the action moves directly toward the climax. A deeper element is the principle of alternation or rhythm, which relates the definite to the complex. The mind of Delano alternates steadily between mistrust and reassurance. It wanders, but wanders in a pattern. The deck of the *San Dominick* strikes him with wonder, with its noisy crowd of blacks, its oakum pickers, its wild Ashantis. But this confusion is attributed to abnormal circumstances, in which discipline has naturally slackened. The strangeness of Cereno is explainable from his sufferings. At one point Cereno confers aside with his

[10] Compare Hawthorne, "Rappaccini's Daughter." The observer, Giovanni, has very much the same problem as Delano, and the use of ambiguity in the two stories presents close parallels.

servant, then asks some highly suspicious questions about the weapons and manning of Delano's ship. But the very crudeness of the questioning disarms suspicion. "To solicit such information openly of the chief person endangered, and so, in effect, setting him on his guard; how unlikely a procedure was that." Delano's misgivings gradually rise in intensity, but, until the end, are allayed. Thus, finally emerging from the Spaniard's cabin to leave the ship, he had got to the point of fearing to be murdered in the passageway. But his fears vanish as soon as he reaches the deck.

This alternation of feeling has a corresponding rhythm in Cereno, who moves consistently between opposite moods. "The singular alternations of courtesy and ill-breeding in the Spanish captain were unaccountable, except on one of two suppositions [both wrong]—innocent lunacy, or wicked imposture." In one phase Don Benito is ceremonious, in the other he withdraws into gloomy indifference, regardless of his guest. At some moments he seems overcome; at others he puts on a rigid self-command.

Critics have commented upon the atmosphere of nightmarish unreality with which Melville invests the *San Dominick*. This atmosphere is in keeping with the theme. The strangeness of the ship is an element of the soul's delusion. Certain motifs and images, however, recur, suggesting that this nightmare has a structure and a meaning. The skill which isolates and focuses the scene is directed toward something more crucial than merely theatrical emphasis:

Always upon boarding a large and populous ship at sea, especially a foreign one, with a nondescript crew such as Lascars or Manilla men, the impression varies in a peculiar way from that produced by first entering a strange house with strange inmates in a strange land. Both house and ship—the one by its walls and blinds, the other by its high bulwarks like ramparts—hoard from view their interiors till the last moment: but in the case of the ship there is this addition; that the living spectacle it contains, upon its sudden and complete disclosure, has, in contrast with the blank ocean which zones it, something of the effect of enchantment. The ship seems unreal; these strange costumes, gestures, and faces, but a shadowy tableau just emerged from the deep, which directly must receive back what it gave.

The advantages of this effect are obvious enough, but by emphasizing the strangeness and isolation, it also can image the mind which perceives them. Delano is removed from all his customary associations, his supports, his criteria. Some have maintained that his slowness amounts to plain stupidity, seriously damaging the story. Certainly the problem is inherent in the theme, which depends upon a balance of uncertainty and knowledge. The eventual revelation of truth must be inevitable; probably the hero will always seem slow in learning the truth. And if he seems *too* slow, the story is ruined. Therefore it is worthwhile reasserting that Melville has dealt with this difficulty. Delano has one vital disability, clearly stated and essential to the meaning of "Benito Cereno." He is "a person of a singularly undistrustful good nature, not liable except on extraordinary and repeated incentives, and hardly then, to indulge in personal alarms, any way involving the imputation of malign evil in man." He does not understand "of what humanity is capable." Beyond this, the problem is real. It is the creation of a complex and malignant mind, a "hive of subtlety," which has deliberately contrived its confusions.

"Benito Cereno" has a decorative color scheme of white, black, and gray.[11] As in the isolation of the ship, this use of color motifs has both an immediate function of design and along with it a deeper significance in theme. In Delano's search for truth the white is good, the black is evil, the gray the ambiguity between them. The first color is quite fittingly gray, for the *San Dominick* is a ship of mystery.

The morning was one peculiar to that coast. Everything was mute and calm; everything was gray. The sea, though undulated into long roods of swells, seemed fixed, and was sleeked at the surface like waved lead that has cooled and set in the smelter's mouth. The sky seemed a gray surtout. Flights of troubled gray fowl, kith and kin with troubled gray vapors among which they were mixed, skimmed low and fitfully over the waters, as swallows over meadows before storms. Shadows present, foreshadowing deeper shadows to come.

Out of these vapors comes wandering the fateful *San Dominick*. Against the gray she looks "like a white-washed monastery after a thunder-storm"; peering over the bulwarks are what seem to be "throngs of dark cowls; while, fitfully revealed through the open port-holes, other

11 See Williams. Professor Williams' comments upon the theme of Church and State, upon the interrelationships of Delano, Cereno, and Babo, and upon primitivism in the Negroes are also valuable.

dark moving figures were dimly described, as of Black Friars pacing the cloisters." The black is evil; the white is good, since we take the side of the whites and accept the verdict of a white court of law. This symbolism of white and black Matthiessen has called "unfortunate in raising unanswered questions," since the Negroes are the victims of social injustice. The failure to answer these questions makes the tragedy, "for all its prolonged suspense, comparatively superficial."[12]

The charge is a crucial one. It is a true one, if we require that tragedy convey an ideal order. There is none such in "Benito Cereno." Melville's symbols, however, are complex and supply a self-criticism of their own. Melville was certainly conscious of the problem. The white is good, but it is also decay and death—a fate deserved from self-neglect and inertia. "As the whale-boat drew more and more nigh, the cause of the peculiar pipe-clayed aspect of the stranger was seen in the slovenly neglect pervading her. The spars, ropes, and great part of the bulwarks, looked woolly, from long unacquaintance with the scraper, tar, and the brush. Her keel seemed laid, her ribs put together, and she launched, from Ezekiel's Valley of Dry Bones." These images are not accidental. They bear a theme and lead directly to the revelation, the unveiling of the figurehead. At the moment of climax, the slaves cut the cable to flee. The end of it whips off a canvas shroud and reveals a white human skeleton—the skeleton of Don Alexandro Aranda, owner of the slaves and friend of Cereno.

Upon this theme of whiteness the black makes his com-

[12] *American Renaissance*, 508.

ment. Beneath the skeleton is chalked the inscription, "Follow your leader!" This is ironically addressed to the white man, but also to the white ship—white with decay. It is not unimportant that the skeleton has been substituted for "the ship's proper figure-head—the image of Christopher Colon, the discoverer of the New World," with its connotation of energy, freedom, youth, and hope. Aranda was killed by the blacks to assure their liberty, and his skeleton was set up to remind the whites to keep their faith—an oath of assistance of course extorted by force and fear. The Negro Babo has his say on whiteness. At the trial Cereno deposes that "the negro Babo showed him a skeleton . . . that the negro Babo asked him whose skeleton that was, and whether, from its whiteness, he should not think it a white's . . . that the same morning the negro Babo took by succession each Spaniard forward, and asked him whose skeleton that was, and whether, from its whiteness, he should not think it a white's; that each Spaniard covered his face." Babo's revenge goes far beyond the provocation. Yet he is partially justified within the theme of whiteness.

Order is important in "Benito Cereno." "In armies, navies, cities, or families, in nature herself, nothing more relaxes good order than misery." "Wonted to the quiet orderliness of the sealer's comfortable family of a crew, the noisy confusion of the *San Dominick's* suffering host repeatedly challenged his [Delano's] eye." " 'Events have not been favorable to much order in my arrangements,' " says Cereno. " 'The negro Babo appointed the four aged negroes . . . to keep what domestic order they could on the decks.' " " 'Had such a thing happened on board the

*Bachelor's Delight,* instant punishment would have followed,' " says Captain Delano. The primary order of "Benito Cereno" is the order of Spain, a hierarchical system in which Church and State are one. The *San Dominick* is a symbol of this order and its fate.

The *San Dominick* is "a very large, and, in its time, a very fine vessel, such as in those days were at intervals encountered along that main; sometimes superseded Acapulco treasure-ships, or retired frigates of the Spanish king's navy, which, like superannuated palaces, still, under a decline of masters, preserved signs of former state." Once a warship, the vessel's teeth have been drawn. "The ship's general model and rig appeared to have undergone no material change from their original warlike and Froissart pattern. However, no guns were seen." "At present neither men nor cannon were seen, though huge ring-bolts and other rusty iron fixtures of the woodwork hinted of twenty-four pounders." The *San Dominick* has a state cabin and state balconies, once splendid but now abandoned and dead. "His glance fell upon the row of small, round dead-lights—closed like coppered eyes of the coffined—and the state-cabin door, once connecting with the gallery, even as the dead-lights had once looked out upon it, but now calked fast like a sarcophagus-lid." Delano speculates that "that state-cabin and this state-balcony had heard the voices of the Spanish king's officers, and the forms of the Lima viceroy's daughters had perhaps leaned where he stood." Delano looks down to the ship's water line, leaning upon the balustrade of the balcony. Below him he sees ribbon grass, "straight as a border of green box; and parterres of sea-weed, broad ovals and crescents, floating nigh and far, with what seemed long formal alleys between, crossing the terraces of swells, and sweeping round as if leading to the grottoes below." The balustrade itself seems "the charred ruin of some summerhouse in a grand garden long running to waste." Here is the formal grandeur of the old regime, and its decadence. Delano leans too heavily upon the balustrade; it gives way and nearly pitches him into the sea.

Benito Cereno is dressed with singular but outmoded richness, in smallclothes and stockings. "There was a certain precision in his attire curiously at variance with the unsightly disorder around; especially in the belittered Ghetto, forward of the mainmast, wholly occupied by the blacks." He wears "a slender sword, silver mounted," the emblem of rule. This sword is in reality an empty hilt in an artificially stiffened scabbard. Cereno's cabin is in disorder. "Part of it had formerly been the quarters of the officers; but since their death all the partitionings had been thrown down." It now resembles "the wide, cluttered hall of some eccentric bachelor-squire in the country." Amid the clutter are "four or five old muskets," an old table with a thumbed missal on it, and over it a small crucifix. Under the table is "a dented cutlass or two, with a hacked harpoon, among some melancholy old rigging, like a heap of poor friar's girdles." There are two settees "of Malacca cane, black with age, and uncomfortable to look at as inquisitor's racks," with an armchair which, because it is supplied with a barber's crotch, "seemed some grotesque engine of torture." There is an open flag locker which reveals various flags in disorder, and a cumbrous washstand of black mahogany "with a pedestal like a font." Finally there is Cereno's bed, "a torn hammock of stained grass . . . the sheets tossed, and the pillow wrinkled up like a brow, as if whoever slept here slept but illy." The cabin is a microcosm of the old Spanish order, fallen now in confusion. It figures forth its warlike power, its spiritual strength, its traditional loyalties—and its inquisitorial rigors. It is also the unhappy chaos of the soul of Cereno. This cabin, a place of actual events, is counterpointed against the state cabin and the balconies, undisturbed relics of the past. Here is the cluttered hall, still occupied; there the palace, dead but unaltered.

The *San Dominick* is massive. Its physical bulk, however, merges with the ambiguities of its meaning. About its great masts are "groves of rigging," which mirror in their complexity the maze in which Delano is wandering. A Spanish sailor seems to gesture to him, "but immediately as if alarmed by some advancing step along the deck within, vanished into *the recesses of the hempen forest, like a poacher.*" This ambiguity can be moral. The corroded mainchains, "of an ancient style, massy and rusty in link, shackle and bolt . . . seemed even more fit for the ship's present business [slaving] than the one for which she had been built." In the midst of the sternpiece, carved with the arms of Castile and Leon, is a device of mysterious significance: "uppermost and central . . . was a dark satyr in a mask, holding his foot on the prostrate neck of a writhing figure, likewise masked."

The *San Dominick* is the old order of Western civilization. This order is solidly grounded in fundamental loyalties and faiths; it is complex and profound. Deeply set in man's spirit, it is worthy of reverence. But in Cereno's

cabin the settees are like inquisitor's racks, and the armchair resembles an instrument of torture. These spiritual
depths have their dark places, this order its sins. The
massive chains are well fitted for slaving.

The old order was made for a "man of war world,"[13]
in which evil perpetually threatens. Like the organization
of a warship's company, its tightly formed hierarchies
were framed for emergencies. The successful revolt of the
slaves is a sign of the system's decay. It was possible because the Negroes were left unchained, by order of their
master, Aranda. But as a slaveowner what had he to do
with kindness and indulgence? The original sin has been
committed: he must either reject it completely or else
adhere strictly to the terms of his tenure. Melville com-
pares the *San Dominick* to a "transatlantic emigrant ship,
among whose multitude of living freight are some individuals, doubtless, as little troublesome as crates and
bales; but the friendly remonstrances of such with their
ruder companions are of not so much avail as the un-
friendly arm of the mate. What the *San Dominick* wanted
was, what the emigrant ship has, stern superior officers."[14]
What the order has now is the ceremony without the substance of power, and insight without the faculty of action.
It has looked too long in the face of evil, and at last grown
unnerved. Its proper symbol is now a monk.

Delano's first sight of the *San Dominick* suggests to him
"a white-washed monastery after a thunderstorm." The
slaves peering over the bulwarks are Black Friars—Do-
minicans. It has been remarked that "Benito" is a Bene-

---

13 See *White-Jacket,* esp. "The End."
14 See "The Emigrants," *Redburn,* chap. 51.

dictine's cloak;[15] and "benito" is derived from "bene-dictus." Shut in his ship's walls, Cereno is like "some hypochondriac abbot" too long cloistered; his manner is like "his imperial countryman's Charles V, just previous to the anchoritish retirement of that monarch from the throne." At the end Don Benito retires to the monastery "on Mount Agonia," accompanied by "one special guardian and consoler, by night and by day." This inseparable companion is the monk *Infelez*.

In Melville, the monk, seeing too well that the world is evil, is forced to retire from it. He is not a bachelor, but has wedded reality all too closely—and Benito is a benedict. A bachelor is a man who would keep his freedom; if necessary he will close his eyes and heart in order to avoid entanglement. The bachelor shuns real commitments. Melville has drawn two kinds of bachelors. One kind believes that the world is wholly and simply bad. But, since this is so, the bachelor need have no traffic with it; it does not engage him deeply. Such a man is the Missouri Bachelor of *The Confidence-Man*, "A Hard Case," who has "no confidence in boys, no confidence in men, no confidence in nature." St. Augustine on Original Sin is his textbook. His universal pessimism is, however, shallow, since he has not paid the price of wisdom. He is justly dismissed as "less a man-hater than a man-hooter."[16] The other and more frequent type is the merry bachelor who shuts his eyes to evil and pain. He believes that men can be happy at the slight expense of a little common-

15 See Feltenstein, "Melville's 'Benito Cereno,'" *American Literature*, Vol. XIX (November, 1947). Miss Feltenstein notes that the name is spelled "Bonito" in the source.
16 Chaps. 21–24.

sense and foresight. The bachelor is competent and canny; he often succeeds in leading a pleasant and tranquil life. Now and then, however, he runs into more things than are dreamt of in his philosophy. Such is the narrator of "Bartleby," who finds through his strange clerk that some ills are cureless. And such is Captain Delano of the *Bachelor's Delight*.

Among the ships in *Moby Dick*, the most fortunate is the *Bachelor*, a "glad ship of good luck." When the *Pequod* encounters her, her hold is full of oil. The crew is in the act of hurling her now useless tryworks into the sea, while the mates and harpooners are dancing with "the olive-hued girls who had eloped with them from the Polynesian Isles." Hailed for news of the white whale, her captain answers, "[I] only heard of him; but don't believe in him at all." Ahab's judgment of the *Bachelor* is concise: "Thou art too damned jolly. Sail on."[17] Stubb, the second mate of the *Pequod,* is a typical merry bachelor. "Good-humored, easy, and careless, he presided over his whale-boat as if the most deadly encounter were but a dinner, and his crew all invited guests."[18]

Melville is most explicit in "The Tartarus of Maids" and "The Paradise of Bachelors." In the first, the narrator visits a paper mill in a remote New England mountain valley. It is the dead of winter, and the factory is bitterly

[17] "The Pequod Meets the Bachelor," chap. 115.

[18] "Knights and Squires," chap. 27. Stubb immunizes himself from the world by his pipe. "I say this continual smoking must have been one cause, at least, of his peculiar disposition; for every one knows that this earthly air, whether ashore or afloat, is terribly inflicted with the nameless miseries of the numberless mortals who have died exhaling it" *(ibid.).*

cold. Shivering girls are tending complicated machines, which strangely suggest the female sexual organs and the process of gestation. The maid, helplessly exposed to the elemental realities, gets from them nothing but suffering; the girls go thinly clothed in the terrible cold. The manager of the mill, a "dark-complexioned, well-wrapped personage," they call Old Bach. Neither bachelors nor maids live fully, but while the maids are victims of life, the bachelors are exempt from it.

In the contrast piece, the narrator attends a bachelor dinner at the Temple, a London Inn of Court. Food, drink, and talk are of the best, and everyone is carefree. "You could plainly see that these easy-hearted men had no wives or children to give an anxious thought." In a really deplorable outburst the narrator exclaims, "Ah! when I bethink me of the sweet hours there passed, enjoying such genial hospitality beneath those time-honored roofs, my heart only finds due utterance through poetry; and with a sigh, I softly sing, 'Carry me back to old Virginny!'" Since these bachelors live in the Temple, they are monastic templars, and this monasticism suggests the contrast of the bachelor and the monk.

The thing called pain, the bugbear styled trouble—those two legends seemed preposterous to their bachelor imaginations. How could men of liberal sense, ripe scholarship in the world, and capacious philosophical and convivial understandings—how could they suffer themselves to be imposed upon by such monkish fables? Pain? Trouble! As well talk of Catholic miracles. No such thing.

Captain Amasa Delano is a good specimen of the

bachelor. He is able and benevolent. When he at last learns the secret of the *San Dominick,* he deals with it effectively—more effectively, in fact, than if he had understood it better. Cereno the monk and Delano the bachelor are complementary, mutually dependent. Cereno, knowing all, has preserved Delano by staying passive; Delano, knowing little, has acted to rescue the Spaniard.

"Had I [says Cereno] dropped the least hint, made the least advance towards an understanding between us, death, explosive death—yours and mine—would have ended the scene."
"True, true," cried Captain Delano, starting, "you have saved my life, Don Benito, more than I yours; saved it, too, against my knowledge and will."
"Nay, my friend," rejoined the Spaniard, courteous even to the point of religion, "God charmed your life, but you saved mine. To think of some things you did—those smilings and chattings, rash pointings and gesturings. For less than these, they slew my mate, Raneds; but you had the Prince of Heaven's safe-conduct through all ambuscades."
"Yes, all is owing to Providence, I know; but the temper of my mind that morning was more than commonly pleasant, while the sight of so much suffering, more apparent than real, added to my good-nature, compassion, and charity, happily interweaving the three. Had it been otherwise, doubtless, as you hint, some of my interferences might have ended unhappily enough. Besides, those feelings I spoke of enabled me to get the better of momentary distrust, at times when acuteness might have cost me my life, without saving another's."

But it needs to be pointed out that Cereno, although otherwise passive, has taken the one crucial action of leaping into Delano's boat—for the sake of the American as much as for himself. Only so could Delano be undeceived in time.

Captain Delano believes in a beneficent Providence. Himself well disposed, he expects no harm; it would be atheistical to doubt that good men are protected. "I to be murdered here at the ends of the earth, on board a haunted pirate-ship by a horrible Spaniard? Too nonsensical to think of! Who would murder Amasa Delano? His conscience is clean. There is some one above." The order of Delano is the order of the *Bachelor's Delight*—a common-sense order, comfortable and quiet. The crew of the *Bachelor's Delight* is easily governed by its good-natured but decisive captain. One golden rule solves all problems —keep them busy. " 'I should think, Don Benito [says the American captain] . . . that you would find it advantageous to keep all your blacks employed, especially the younger ones, no matter at what useless task, and no matter what happens to the ship. Why, even with my little band, I find such a course indispensable.' "

The practical Delano, believing as he does in his simple Providence, which he is inclined to associate with the order of nature, is able to save alive the body of Cereno but cannot help his soul. He has little notion of the effect of malignant evil upon the Spaniard's deeper spirit. The world is good, and, accidental ills now happily removed, what then remains?


"But the past is passed; why moralize upon it? Forget it. See, yon bright sun has forgotten it all, and the blue sea, and the blue sky; these have turned over new leaves."

"Because they have no memory," he dejectedly replied; "because they are not human."

"But these mild trades that now fan your cheek, do they not come with a human-like healing to you? Warm friends, steadfast friends are the trades."

"With their steadfastness they but waft me to my tomb, Senor," was the foreboding response.

"You are saved," cried Captain Delano, more and more astonished and pained: "you are saved: what has cast such a shadow upon you?"

"The negro."

What is "the negro"? After his rescue Cereno will not board the *Bachelor's Delight* until the Negro Babo has been taken below. "Nor then, nor at any time after, would he look at him." Babo is the symbol of the slaves, one kind of blackness. With a wider reference he is everything untamed and demoniac—the principle of unknown terror. Like the White Whale, he stands for "that intangible malignity which has been from the beginning; to whose dominion even the modern Christians ascribe one-half of the worlds."[19] Babo is the shark beneath the waters. Melville, describing sharks tearing at the body of a dead sperm whale, remarks, "If you have never seen that sight, then suspend your decision about the propriety of devil-worship, and the expediency of conciliating the devil."[20] He is "the demonism in the world," which the Vermont colt snuffs in the buffalo robe.[21]

Babo is not quite, however, the motiveless malignity of Iago, who must invent the reasons for his wickedness. Cor-

[19] "Moby Dick," *Moby Dick,* chap. 41.
[20] "Stubb's Supper," chap. 64.
[21] "The Whiteness of the Whale," chap. 42.

respondingly, he is not quite Claggart, the master-at-arms of "Billy Budd," who is a pure evil according to nature. For he has been oppressed by social order, and not only by the white man's. " 'Poor Babo here, in his own land, was only a poor slave; a black man's slave was Babo, who now is the white's.' " Therefore, while from one point of view Babo is Satan, an absolute principle of destruction, a pure hatred of all order, he is likewise a sufferer from order, its prober and test, the sign of its weakness. In this aspect he is the vengeance of nature, evoked by the inequities of all orders. When they transgress too far against nature, the vengeance beats them down.

Babo is thus in part the symbol of the slaves, whose blackness is the destructive vigor of the primitive. But he goes beyond their natural savagery—even beyond the fierceness of the untamed Ashantis. They have had their own simpler order, and their revolt is their attempt to return to it. The giant Atufal was a king in his own country, and significantly counterbalances the deeper, more equivocal Babo.

The source of the action is Babo's revolt. Thus the *San Dominick* which Delano sees is a malign parody of the original system, in which the real power conceals itself behind animated puppets. Since the truth cannot wholly be hidden, Babo tries to confuse it. Further, going beyond the necessities of the situation, Babo deliberately desecrates the sanctities of the old faith and rule.

He plays the role of the loyal, solicitous servant, the shadow of Cereno, while secretly ruling the ship. One ironic effect of this device is to make Cereno appear an absolute monarch of godlike pride and assumption.

"Proud as he was moody, he condescended to no personal mandate. Whatever special orders were necessary, their delivery was delegated to his body-servant." This equivocal association of master and servant has a more vital result: it diverts the suspicions of Delano always to Cereno, concealing from him their true source. In addition, Babo has arranged the elaborate mockery by which the former king Atufal appears before Cereno at stated hours in chains, to which the latter alone has the key. In reality the chains can be instantly thrown aside, but the innocent Delano begs that the punishment be remitted. He is so thoroughly deceived as to say, " 'For all the license you permit in some things, I fear lest at bottom, you are a bitter hard master.' " He misinterprets Cereno's response: "Again Don Benito shrank; and this time, as the good sailor thought, from a genuine twinge of his conscience."

The true state of things cannot completely be hidden. A Spanish lad is assaulted by a slave boy; a sailor is trampled by two Negroes; these incidents are difficult to explain. Against the restraining and concealing agency of the four old oakum pickers, whom Babo has appointed to keep order, are the six Ashantis, who are polishing hatchets. These "sat intent upon their task, except at intervals, when, with the peculiar love in negroes of uniting industry with pastime, two and two they sideways clashed their hatchets together, like cymbals, with a barbarous din." This clashing, which mingles with the action like a chorus, is like a chorus the voice of truth, if Delano could interpret it. At his most suspicious, he has some glimmerings. "By a curious coincidence, as each point was recalled, the black wizards of Ashantis would strike up with their hatchets, as in ominous comment on the white stranger's thoughts."

The Spanish sailors try to communicate with Delano by indirection, under surveillance and at deadly risk. Thus he comes upon an old seaman working a knot, with some blacks obligingly holding the strands of the rope. This knot, a most extraordinary artifice, is strangely like Delano's present state of mind, which passes

by a not uncongenial transition . . . from its own entanglements to those of the hemp. For intricacy, such a knot he had never seen in an American ship, nor indeed any other. The old man looked like an Egyptian priest, making Gordian knots for the temple of Ammon. The knot seemed a combination of double-blowing-knot, treble-crown-knot, back-handed-well-knot, knot-in-and-out-knot, and jamming-knot.

At last, puzzled to comprehend the meaning of such a knot, Captain Delano addressed the knotter:—

"What are you knotting there, my man?"

"The knot," was the brief reply, without looking up.

"So it seems; but what is it for?"

"For some one else to undo," muttered back the old man . . . .

While Captain Delano stood watching him suddenly the old man threw the knot towards him, saying . . . something to this effect: "Undo it, cut it, quick."

This is the Gordian knot of the *San Dominick,* too complicated to untie. Delano cannot cut it yet, for he is only dimly aware that the knot exists until Cereno enlightens him. To try to cut it now would be suicide, for he himself is a part of it. He cuts it at last, but this practical solution is inadequate; it will not save the Spaniard. Ideally the knot should be unwound, its relationships fathomed, its intricate mazes traced back to their beginnings. It is the tragedy of "Benito Cereno" that this real solution is impossible. Could a deeper man than Delano have found the deep truth? Melville makes us consider this question, but the symbol itself says no; the problem is beyond the human intellect. There is an interesting sequel to this episode. It causes the old sailor's death, as we later learn, for the watchers suspect something. He is quietly escorted below and there done away with. But the suspicions are simpler than the truth; it is thought that the knot conceals a written message. The blacks, too, cut the knot in their fashion.

Babo intentionally desecrates the old order of the Spaniards, combining, as it were, pleasure with business. In a remarkable scene in the cabin, he forces Cereno to wear the flag of Spain for a barber's apron. The situation gets much of its power from the incongruity of Delano's interpretation of it. Babo is shaving his master, while the American captain looks on. Fond of Negroes, to whom he takes "not philanthropically but genially, just as other men to Newfoundland dogs," Delano is both delighted and amused by the spectacle of the faithful Negro servant. "Among other things, he was amused by an odd instance of the African love of bright colors and fine shows, in the black's informally taking from the flag-locker a great piece of bunting of all hues, and lavishly tucking it under his master's chin for an apron." The shaving proceeds. Don Benito is strangely nervous of the bright blade, and in his agitation he loosens a corner of the apron, revealing the castle and the lion of Spain. Delano takes this as a harmless piece of naïveté: " 'It's well it's only I, and not the King, that sees this . . . but'—turning towards the black—'It's all one, I suppose, so the colors be gay'; which playful remark did not fail somewhat to tickle the negro." In another of the slaves this impropriety might have come from ignorance or sheer indifference. In the subtle Babo it is purposeful, and making Cereno participate in the action is a refinement of cruelty.

The shaving of Don Benito is a ritual murder. The description suggests one interpretation by which the implements of Spanish cruelty are turned against the Spaniard, although this theme is merely latent. It is strengthened, however, by the deliberate contrast of black and white. "The mode of shaving among the Spaniards is a little different from what it is with other nations. They have a basin . . . which on one side is scooped out, so as accurately to receive the chin." This basin resembles a headsman's block. Cereno, his head imprisoned by the basin, shudders at the sight of the razor. "His usual ghastliness was heightened by the lather, which lather, again, was intensified in its hue by the contrasting sootiness of the negro's body. Altogether the scene was somewhat peculiar, at least to Captain Delano, nor, as he saw the two thus postured, could he resist the vagary, that in the black he saw a headsman, and in the white a man at the block." One remembers that the washstand is like a font and finds a baptismal consecration and dedication in the ministrations of Babo, which lead toward a sacrifice. "The shaving over, the servant bestirred himself with a small bottle of scented waters, pouring a few drops on the head, and then diligently rubbing; the vehemence of the exercise causing the muscles of his face to twitch rather strangely." The Spaniard is anointed, clipped, and combed, a process which he bears "like any resigned gentleman in barber's hands . . . indeed, he sat so pale and rigid now, that the negro seemed a Nubian sculptor finishing off a white statue-head." The last Spaniard to undergo Babo's attentions had been Don Alexandro Aranda, whose white skeleton is now the *San Dominick's* figurehead.

No order in "Benito Cereno" is intended to represent the ideal: not the spiritual order of Cereno, nor the practical order of Delano, not the perverse order of Babo, a parasite which battens on the system that conceals it. And, although Melville suggests broader implications than any of these orders contain, there is no clear ideal to be found by synthesizing them. The highest standard, the revered tradition of Church and State, is a limited and "horological"[22] system, exposed to the severest criticism of the common-sense American Delano and convicted of oppression by Babo. In "Billy Budd," another horological story, the ideal is embodied in Captain Vere, who distinguishes the necessities of practice from the values of absolute justice. Billy Budd must die for killing his superior officer; but at the Day of Judgment Billy Budd will be vindicated.

If, then, tragedy portrays the ideal order, "Benito Cereno" cannot claim to be tragedy. If it is conceived, however, as the realization of mystery, the effective presentment of overwhelming complexity, one's verdict will be different. For the chief virtue of "Benito Cereno" is its

[22] See "The Journey and the Pamphlet," *Pierre*, Bk. XIV.

sense of an unknown so powerful that it rivals Fate. The man of practical good will, the efficient and officious Delano, can do little to combat it.

Of the orders of the story, Cereno's is the most profound. Melville is Delano as well as Cereno, however, and we see through Delano's eyes. Reality is scanned from the vantage point of the practical, optimistic, liberal nineteenth century.[23] Whatever its shortcomings, it is after all in possession; it exists and is efficacious; whatever the virtues of Cereno's order, in the actual world it is fading. The order of the Negroes, if we omit the elements of absolute evil in Babo, raises the question of primitivism. The Negroes are not the primitives of *Typee's* happy valley, for their problems are more explosive. Crisis arouses in them the same elemental savagery as flashes momentarily in *Typee* in the fierce chief Mow-Mow. In "Benito Cereno," the verdict on the primitive is unfavorable. The rebellious slaves are good and also evil, like other men, but they lack a principle of control. Natural goodness is no better thought of than in *Moby Dick* in the cook's sermon to the sharks: " 'Your woraciousness, fellow-critters, I don't blame ye so much for; dat is natur, and can't be helped; but to gobern dat

[23] "In *Bartleby* and in *Benito Cereno* we find Melville identifying himself with two figures. The first is the upper-middle-class Anglo-Saxon American, sound in moral principle, mediocre in spiritual development, a successful and respectable citizen . . . . The second figure, the spiritual man, is Bartleby and Benito Cereno" (Chase. *Herman Melville,* 148). Chase goes on to compare the relationship of Delano and Cereno to the Freudian relationship of father and son. It would be profitable to examine the resemblances to Christopher Newman and Claire de Cintré in Henry James's *The American.*

wicked natur, dat is de pint. You is sharks, sartin; but if you gobern de shark in you, why den you be angel; for all angel is not'ing more dan de shark well goberned.' "[24] The Negroes are not well governed.

Delano expounds the doctrine of primitivism: the Negro is natural harmony and joy. He has "a certain easy cheerfulness, harmonious in every glance and gesture; as though God had set the whole negro to some pleasant tune." He is, like Hawthorne's Donatello, in tune with nature, a man who has somehow escaped the Fall and the separation. So Delano is delighted by the sight of a young Negress with her child. "There's naked nature, now; pure tenderness and love, thought Captain Delano, well pleased"; and goes on to reflect on the combined tenderness and toughness of savage women, "unsophisticated as leopardesses; loving as doves." But the captain's observations are drawn from the evil Babo, and, as for the women, the court depositions show them crueler than the men. They "would have tortured to death, instead of simply killing, the Spaniards slain by command of the negro Babo."

This harmony and this tenderness really exist, but Delano interprets them too shallowly. The slaves are better and worse than the theory of primitivism. Over them also hangs the shadow of the Fall; and as men they, too, are mysteries. Delano does not know all that human beings are capable of, and he has not allowed for the difficulties of understanding men unlike himself. Without such understanding it is well to be cautious. "However charitable it may be to view Indians as members of the

[24] "Stubb's Supper," chap. 64.

Society of Friends, yet to affirm them such to one ignorant of Indians, whose lonely path lies a long way through their lands, this, in the event, might prove not only injudicious but cruel."[25]

It has been reasonably charged that "Benito Cereno" is insufficiently "worked up" from its source, particularly in its reproduction of Cereno's deposition to the court. The facts of Melville's revision need not be reconsidered here. It may not be entirely valueless, however, to reconsider the nature of the story. In "Benito Cereno," the literal, legal truth of fact is a metaphor for truth of the spirit. The search for the one is implicitly the search for the other. Cereno himself, a broken man withholding himself from retirement and death to testify to the facts, is an appropriate symbol for the quest for truth; and his appropriateness is not lessened by the hint that not all has been told. "Benito" is comparable to the quasi-scientific chapters of *Moby Dick,* which are really an inquiry into the nature, the methods, and the limits of human knowledge.

In the deposition, Melville uses the stately phrases of legal formula to embody a vision of tragic life. Gradually they take on deep cadences, in which Cereno is merged with the public occasion of his testimony, in the frame of his order. "He said that he is twenty-nine years of age, and broken in body and mind; that when finally dismissed by the court, he shall not return home to Chili, but betake himself to the monastery on Mount Agonia

[25] "Containing the Metaphysics of Indian-hating, According to the Views of One Evidently not so Prepossessed as Rousseau in Favour of Savages," *The Confidence-Man,* chap. 26.

without; and signed with his honor, and crossed himself, and, for the time, departed as he came, in his litter, with the monk Infelez, to the Hospital de Sacerdotes." This sentence has the essential quality of "Benito Cereno." Its deepest effects are muted. It has not the life nor the luminescence of *Moby Dick.* Cereno is not Ahab, nor Delano, Ishmael—and Babo is smaller than the whale. It is in the sober vein of the later work, well represented by its colors. But after *Moby Dick* the tale of "Benito Cereno" is Melville's most fully achieved piece of writing.

# Index